ABANDONED PLACES
ABANDONED MEMORIES
APPALACHIAN EDITION

BY

SHARON DAY AND JULIE FERGUSON

Abandoned Places: Abandoned Memories (Appalachian Edition)

DEDICATION

We dedicate this book to all the folks who:
Love historic sites and abandoned buildings
Wonder about the past
Are curious about psychic visions
Would like to learn how buildings carry memories
And
Enjoyed the first book in this series, the "Desert Edition."

We would especially like to thank Junior and Linda Coley who shared a most unique and wonderful location with us, allowing us to access an interior and to share its past with us before it was gone by the wrecking ball. We were honored to be some of the last to photograph it and to immortalize a place of comfort and memories, beauty and all that makes Appalachia so beautiful and cherished.

Abandoned Places: Abandoned Memories (Appalachian Edition)

INTRODUCTION

Psychometry: *A psychic skill of touching an object and getting information of another who has handled the object.*

Our "Abandoned Places: Abandoned Memories" Series began with the Desert Edition and now we are introducing our second in the series based on Appalachian locations.

This is an unusual series of books that were based on a very novel approach – Julie's and my love of urban exploration, her photographic skills and my psychic skills combined.

Julie's photography exposes the bleak present-day look of these abandoned sites and my psychic reads bring to life a moment in time that is no longer, but still leaves its lingering essence for someone who has the skills to bring it to life again, visually and emotionally.

You will find bonuses between each chapter that provide interesting information for those who love abandoned sites, history, lingering ghosts, and more.

We hope you enjoy our series and it is our intention to do more editions in the future as we hit the road and document many places that, as of the writing of this book,

Abandoned Places: Abandoned Memories (Appalachian Edition)

may be no longer. (*Note: As of the publishing of this book, the church, parson's house and the abandoned store have been torn down*).

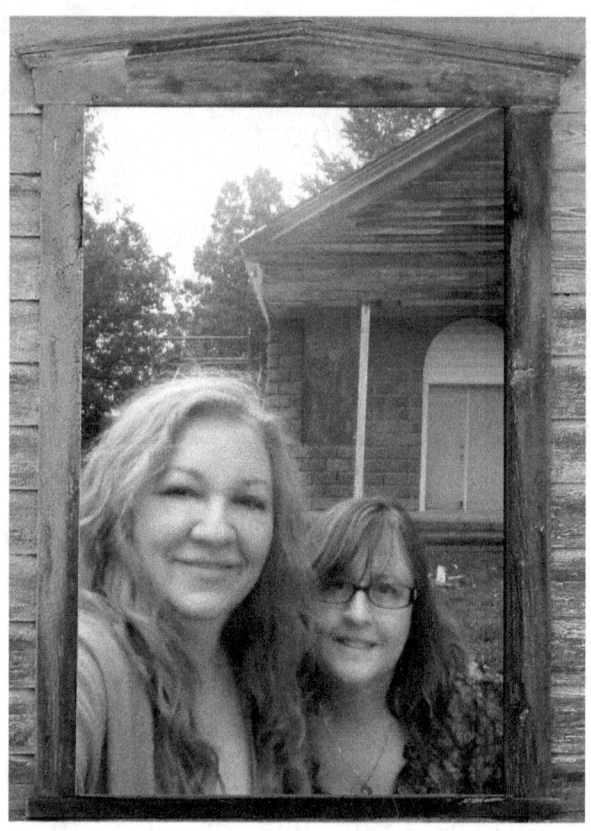

Abandoned Places: Abandoned Memories (Appalachian Edition)

TABLE OF CONTENTS

Abandoned Places: Abandoned Memories (Appalachian Edition)

CHAPTER ONE
ABANDONED SCHOOLHOUSE

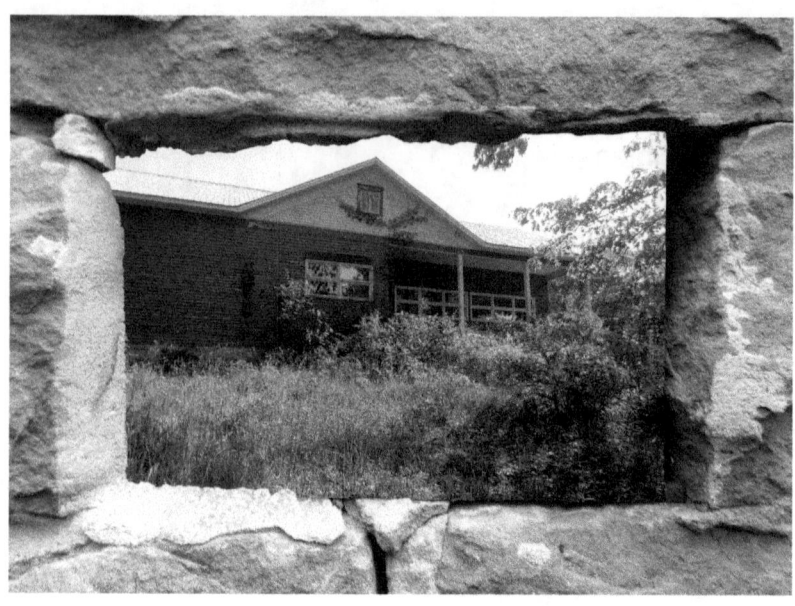

We rounded a bend on a country road in West Virginia to see a bright green meadow unfold dotted with wildflowers and hovering butterflies.

On the hill overlooking the meadow and staring down at an ancient cemetery, sat a little red schoolhouse. Proliferated with bright chartreuse late spring growth, vines, raspberry brambles, and unkempt grasses, it sat wide and squat, faded, but intact, in spite of nature trying to wrestle it back to the earth with thick sinewy arm-like vines.

On a muggy early June morning, Julie and I considered our approach. We wanted to photograph this magnificent relic of a simpler time, but nature was intimidating us with briars and dreaded blood-sucking ticks.

Julie wasn't accustomed to the plant life of the East Coast and overgrown locations, but even so, she didn't flinch wading through the raspberry vines as they clung to her shirt. Her precious camera held high above the thicket, she plunged towards the structure, determined to get up close and photograph it. The look of concentration on her face made me smile. She was passionate about documenting abandoned places and sometimes singularly focused on photographing, so I turned and looked out to be sure no one would approach us unnoticed while she went to her task of capturing the historic old building.

The porch wood was dry, but sturdy enough. Through the huge glass pane windows, we could see a jumble of hip high items from desk chairs and chalkboards to old computers and sewing machines. It looked as if they had used the school as a drop off point for all kinds of other schools' items.

Bees buzzed by us and the damp thick air was taxing on every breath, but we were so thrilled by the victory of making it through the overgrowth that we were only just realizing how the vines were engorging every window until they were almost completely obliterated.

The school was choking to death and we were some of the last witnesses to its imminent demise by neglect.

Julie pressed her nose to the windows and peered inside at the waist high pile of debris, wondering why they would leave it behind and not utilize it in other schools in such an impoverished state.

As she decided how to frame the shots, her eyes were riveted to the vines and the way they engulfed the entire structure, insisting their way into air vents and broken windows, looking for any toe hold. Nature took over structures in a much different way in Appalachia than the desert did. The desert bleached and dried everything like bones of a long-dead animal. In the east, the plants reclaimed the structures to the forests surrounding the building in a kind of architectural mulch.

Butterflies danced wildly around the porch and hovered over berry blossoms, completely oblivious to the lonely structure and the presence of us lingering on the sagging porch.

Julie pivoted and studied the field and distant old cemetery and considered the view these children had each day they attended the small building. It was such a simple and basic schoolhouse and such a glorious setting. If she had been a child there, she thought, the location and having the teacher's undivided attention in small classrooms would have been precious. Some things, school budgets couldn't buy, like clean air and growing up with the same kids and families all around in that comforting way small town neighbors watched out for one another.

We worked our way off the porch, through the brambles, briars and grasses to the side of the building where a back door sat open, bees going in and out enough to know a bee's nest was probably within. Instead of plunging in and being surprised by a nest of wasps, Julie photographed the vines that took over the entire side wall while I wandered, studying the chipped faded red paint turning an almost sad magenta shade, and recalling how it looked 8 years earlier when I had last been there.

My oldest sister, Tina, was in West Virginia for a family reunion and wanted us to drive by the schoolhouse. She had her eye on it and wanted to buy it and renovate it into a cute little home.

Abandoned Places: Abandoned Memories (Appalachian Edition)

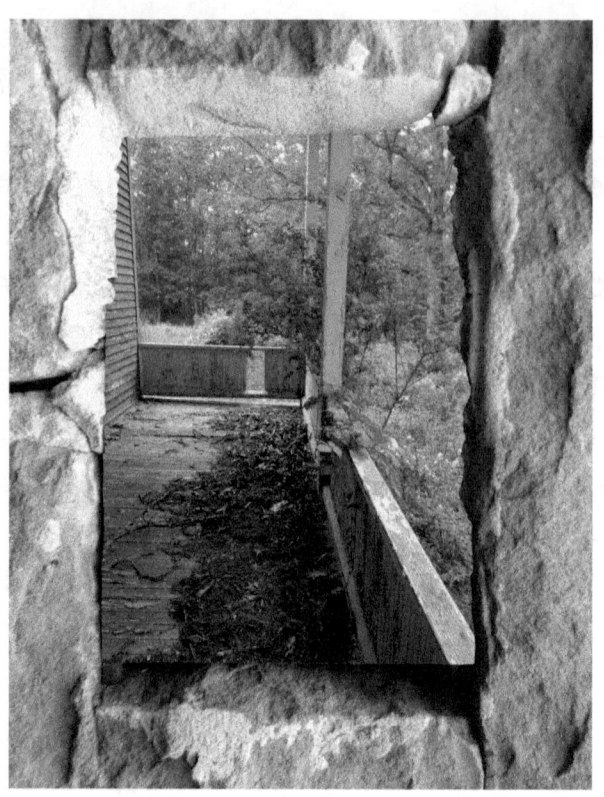

She had died only a month later quite suddenly. The schoolhouse should have made me melancholy, but seeing it still sitting there, contents still intact, no one having torn it down or bought it, made me feel as if it were suspended in time and Tina still existed in the same plane this forgotten building occupied. If one of our last places together was gone, it would have signaled an end of an era. That it remained meant her dream to make it a home could still be a possibility for some insightful person.

Abandoned Places: Abandoned Memories (Appalachian Edition)

I realized a lot had changed since the last time I was there. I was now divorced for 3 years from my 26-year long marriage. This pilgrimage to where my family resided made me put my life in Arizona in perspective and made me ponder how, I was really free to go anywhere and live, something I had grieved for my entire marriage.

I looked at the schoolhouse, imagining it dolled up with bright new red paint, weeds cleared away and some pretty boxwoods, perhaps some nut and fruit trees, a little veggie garden, facing an enormous field, a picturesque cemetery, and a quiet road with no lights and huge stars at night, clean air, and lightning bugs in the summer eves, and wood smoke in the winter.

I also realized I would have no one to talk to, be utterly alone and vulnerable with no police or medical facilities anywhere around, no shops or movie theaters, and few prospects for available middle-aged men for companionship. As beautiful as it was, without someone to share it with, it was just a backdrop.

It was, however, a few moments of fanciful musings realizing how much control I had over my life after a marriage that plotted out every repetitious day of my life for the rest of my existence.

As I rounded the corner to see what Julie was photographing, my eyes went to an old kid's phonograph sitting on the side porch, so lonely and forgotten. When I bent over to touch it, a soul touched my mind and I read it immediately.

Julie clicked off a picture and asked, "is this the item?"

I nodded as my mind sorted out the simplest parts of the reading, sex of the individual, positive, negative, emotions, relationships, attitude and memories.

As we left the location and drove off to the next, my mind wandered back to the read and the thousands of other items still contained within the schoolhouse, each of them carrying the essence of others who had spent only moments in time with them each day and yet left much of their information behind.

But, my mind was attached to this little boy and his story was becoming clear....

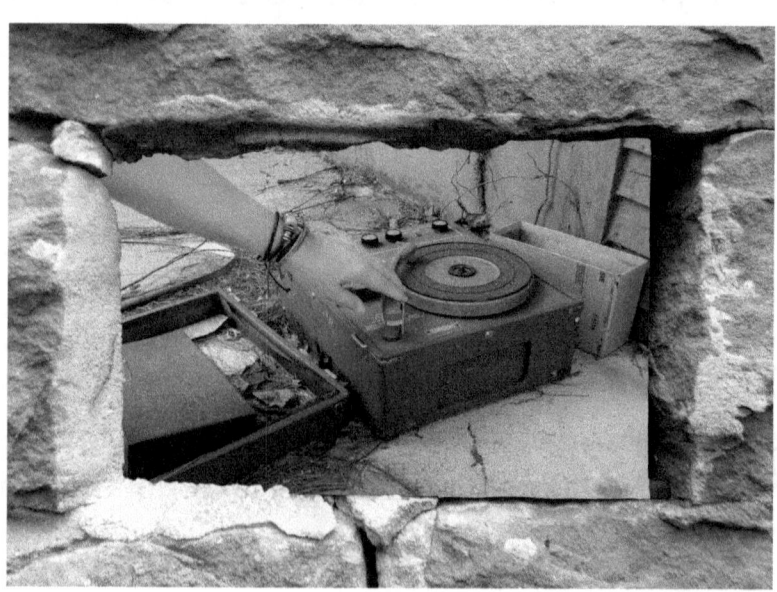

Abandoned Places: Abandoned Memories (Appalachian Edition)

DADDY'S LITTLE MAN

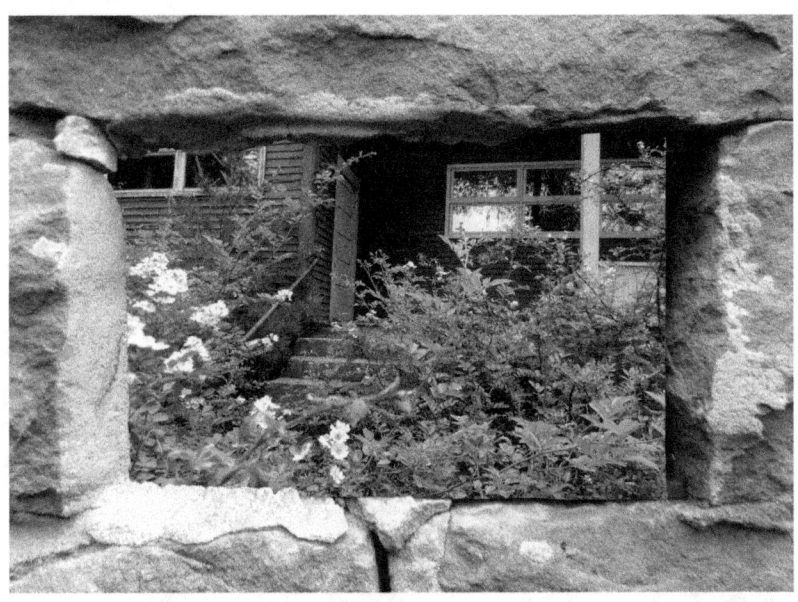

He tried three times to leave the house with his books, but his daddy kept calling him back to the dimly lit living room, windows covered with old sheets because his daddy's eyes got sensitive after the accident. At least, that was what he said when he asked about the change.

"Come 'ere." His daddy's voice wasn't right. His words were slow and he often times forgot what he was going to say. Mama said it was the medicine he took for the pain.

Abandoned Places: Abandoned Memories (Appalachian Edition)

Tommy set down his books with a sigh and went back to see what it was this time. The last two times, his daddy wanted a drink refill and wanted him to find the remote control.

He probably needs more wood in the fireplace that isn't even lit or gonna be lit.

From his recliner, the still powerfully built, but now crippled man, waved his plastic cup at Tommy, without regard for the cherry Kool-Aid contents splashing onto the brown and gold fabric of the chair.

"You be sure an tell yer teacher you expect to have time in the field to work on second base."

"I will, daddy." He waited, sure that his daddy had one more order for him.

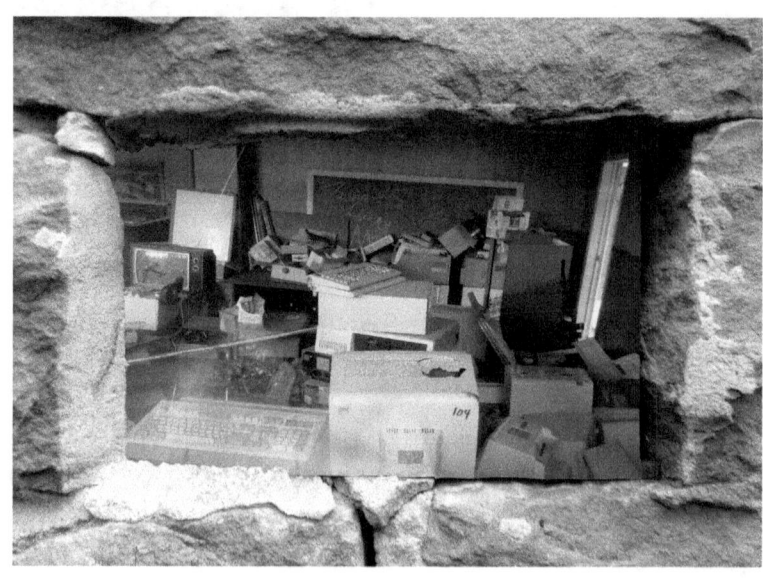

Abandoned Places: Abandoned Memories (Appalachian Edition)

The other six kids had left for school, but Tommy, the youngest, was going to be late once again. Some days, his daddy told him to stay home and he'd give him a sick excuse for missing school. His daddy didn't like being alone and he didn't know what to do with his time now that he couldn't work at his job.

Their mama went to work at a local hotel and Tommy missed her voice, the kiss to the top of his forehead, and her cooking. His oldest sister was an awful cook and he missed his mama requesting beautiful sketches to put on the fridge.

Maybe daddy just misses her too.

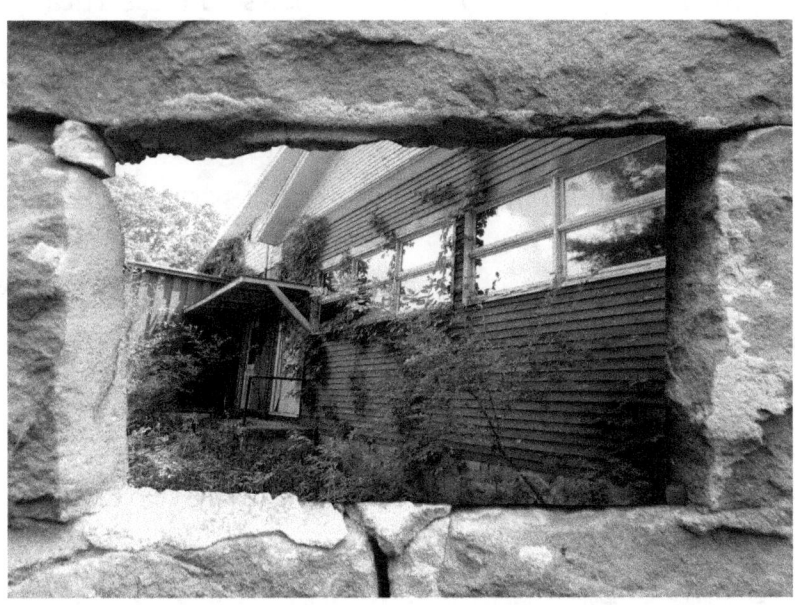

Abandoned Places: Abandoned Memories (Appalachian Edition)

Tommy tried to be patient, but today was a rough one. The teacher had asked him to draw a picture for the classroom door because he was the artist, but Tommy knew dreams of being an artist were all dashed the minute his daddy took a tumble. It was up to the boys to become laborers, not dreamers.

His older brothers already had taken on simple digging and mowing jobs, but his oldest brother was looking for bridge maintenance work and quitting high school. None of them wanted to work the mines, but Tommy knew at some point, their daddy would insist on it. It was hard to say no to a man who commanded the household and determined what it was to be a man.

He was nearly out the door again when his father called out.

"Your mama doesn't want you to go to college."

That stopped Tommy in his tracks to the back door. "Huh?"

His father called through the wall between the kitchen and family room. "None of you are going to college, ya know. There's real world work to be done. None of that is found in those books. Never did fuckin' use algebra." The pills made his voice slower than usual.

"Yes, daddy."

Tommy slipped the books off the kitchen table silently and tiptoed to the door. If he opened it fast enough, he would appear to have not heard his father call him one more time. He knew that the sound of him leaving seemed to make his father almost insecure. It was a side to the big gruff man that confused him greatly.

He held his breath, turned the knob and rushed out into the chilly damp morning air. As he swung the door closed, Tommy heard his father's voice and clicked it shut, racing across the dewy lawn towards the roadway.

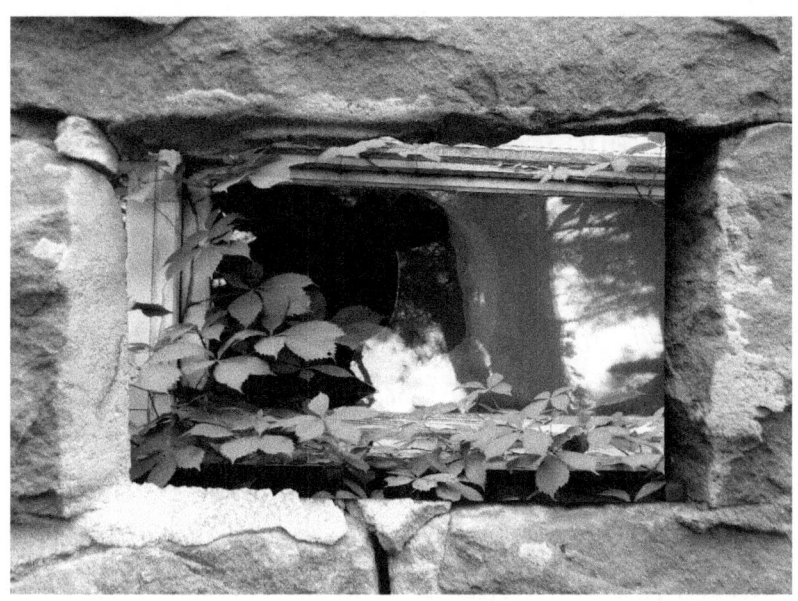

There was no way he could tell his daddy that he had been picked to do art for his classroom when he was supposed to be out playing softball and mastering his position at second base. He also knew that his daddy had him lined up to carry groceries and help their elderly neighbor when she drove into town for supplies. His time

Abandoned Places: Abandoned Memories (Appalachian Edition)

as a kid was coming to a close and his time as a future laborer was beginning.

There were two choices as Tommy saw it; get a scholarship in sports and go away to college and be rich and famous or work at hard labor the rest of his life, never using his paints and brushes, never writing stories about woodland animals and their secret lives in children's books.

It kept him up at night, all these conflicting feelings; feeling guilty for wanting something that was a luxury, being an artist, and the very real world his daddy wanted to prepare him for. He didn't like baseball and he was scrawny compared to his brothers and not built for physical labor. And, asthma made it even worse.

Big baby! Just focus on baseball. Get out of here. Let the others take care of him.

When his belly quivered with fear and doubt, grief and hopelessness, Tommy mentally chewed himself out for being weak. The truth was, his siblings would all leave home before him. He was the last one there. He would be taking care of his mama and daddy the rest of his life. His only chance was to try and get a scholarship and have an excuse that was legitimate enough in his daddy's eyes. His daddy could boast and brag and Tommy could send them money. It seemed the only future available. At least, the only one that didn't make him cry himself to sleep at night.

It was time to give up dreams, like being an artist or writer, having a daddy who was able to work, a mama who stayed at home, and a future that was his own. Now his inner coach reminded him over and over again,

Second base. That's my freedom!
Second base. That's my freedom!
Second base. That's my freedom!

A raccoon shuffled out of the ditch along the road and regarded Tommy for a moment and then looked both ways before crossing. His little hands had been clasped in front of him and the hair around his eyes looked like sunglasses. It inspired Tommy to want to draw one, but then his stomach sank when he realized that wasn't his future. He had to outgrow that silly stuff.

Drawing is for babies. You can't make money at it and you can't get out of here making pictures.

His teacher was waiting out front when he arrived. Tommy tightened his jaw and awaited some complaint. The look on her face showed the fight she always had between encouraging the class as a gentle friend and her role as an example and leader.

"I got your note on my desk about the art work. Why, Tommy?" She reached out to put her hand on his head, but Tommy stepped back.

No coddling anymore.

"I need to practice softball."

"But, Tommy, you're our resident artist."

Abandoned Places: Abandoned Memories (Appalachian Edition)

He looked down at his sneakers, unable to show her the last glimmers of hope in his eyes.

"I don't have time for art anymore. I have more important things to do."

She sighed.

The silence had him glancing back up. Surprisingly, her arms were folded across her chest and her gaze was fixed on the field in the distance.

"I'm sad to hear that, Tommy. You have real talent in art, more so than softball." With that, she pivoted on her heels and went back inside.

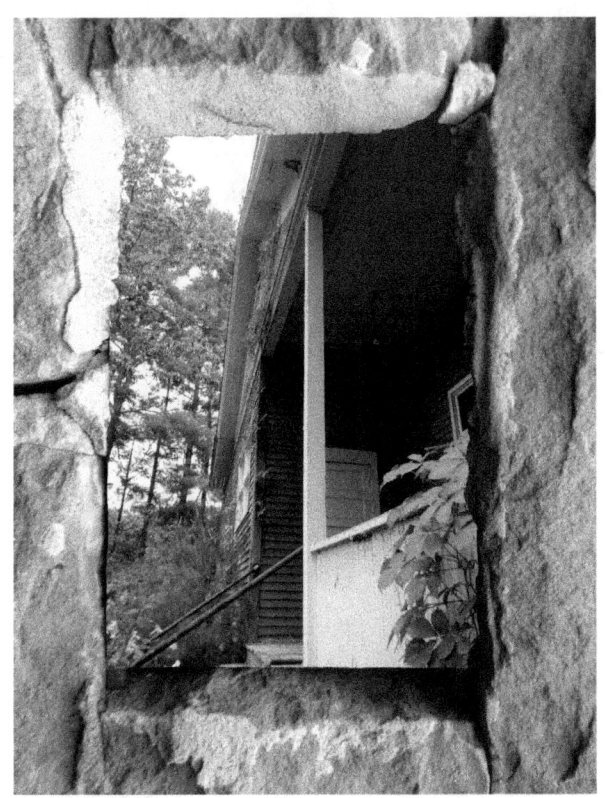

Practice will keep me after school. Less time at home taking care of daddy, more time getting ready for my future. Samantha will probably end up doing the art. Let her do it. She's a girl.

Tommy swung the door open, focusing all his thoughts on softball and the only hope he had left. Instead of noting the way the sunlight came through the bank of windows on the far side of the classroom and made Dorrie's hair like a bright carrot halo, he focused on the baseball glove on the bottom of his desk book holder and

Abandoned Places: Abandoned Memories (Appalachian Edition)

focused his mind, desperately trying to adjust to his new mission.

The glove is better than colored pencils and paper. It's powerful. It's respected. It makes money.

But, somewhere down in the icy cold well of his belly, Tommy knew deep inside that it would never hold the promise and the love that the art tools held.

BONUS
URBAN EXPLORATION
TIPS

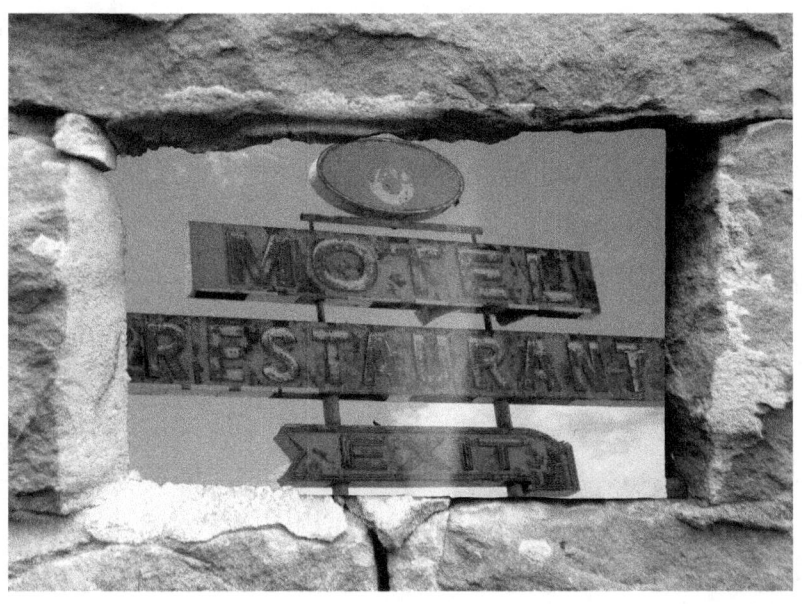

As unique a hobby as urban exploration is, it's also dangerous and sometimes illegal if one doesn't follow posted signs. Here are just some tips that Julie and I have learned over the past several years of pursuing this documentation of buildings (*at least half of which we catalogued are now torn down, including one entire town!*)

Abandoned Places: Abandoned Memories (Appalachian Edition)

Having the right tools is critical. We always suggest you don't even think about embarking on this trek without a tetanus shot. That being said, there are a lot of dangers that come in the form of indigents, drug dealers, bees and animals nesting, weak floor boards, asbestos, glass, and potentially – police arrest.

We carry masks to protect from asbestos and other inhaled dangers like Hantavirus here in the Southwest, where disturbing areas where rodents have peed can have you inhaling something dangerous. Strong gloves are good in case you plan to move something to take a picture. You also will want a flashlight. We've gone into amazing buildings to find they had a basement. Without a flashlight, exploring that would have been impossible and even with a flash on the camera, the flashlight can supplement the lighting for a clearer photo.

There are some basics that are no-nonsense; bringing water, hand wipes, and a cell phone. In an ideal situation, you have 4 people going into these places, two stand facing out to look for oncoming people and animals and two go inside to photograph and account for each other. That way, if one falls through a floorboard, the other witnessed it and can get help.

We always adhere to "No Trespassing" signs. You will be in trouble if you are found by the police or owners and you ignored postings. When no signs are posted, we can get off with a, "*we wanted to photograph this pretty* old place" and are asked to leave with our cameras. You also do not want to cause damage to any site. If you find it locked up and windows tight, photograph the outside.

How do we find these gems?

Julie and I have a policy often times of using Google Earth to scan an area we're driving through beforehand. We look on the outskirts of the town for the industrial areas. We look at rural towns that have died off and mining towns that have dwindled. We can get a good opportunity to narrow down where in the town we want to explore that looks left behind or deteriorating.

In dying towns, the main street area often has emptied shops, but if you go back behind those areas, you find the neighborhoods that died off when the town lost business. We've found this usually starts a few streets down from the main street.

Rural areas with farmhouses and small defunct towns are found more often along alternate freeways and not the main freeway. Along the main freeway, you are likely to find some real gems too in the form of abandoned gas stations and once happy tourists businesses that went under. Some of the most fascinating 1950s roadside motels and cabanas that have been abandoned were along main streets in small highway-dependent towns.

Julie and I went to Tucson one time and along I-10, the main route, there was a town called Picacho. All that was left was the mid century family road trip attraction cheesy motels, gas stations, and such, a little post office, a little community church. The town was mostly abandoned and made for great photographing, but when we went back about a year later, we couldn't find the town. A local told us it had been plowed under. We might have been the last to document it.

We have been chased from abandoned sites by bees and by indigents, so forewarning is critical. Fill your pocket with rocks from the ground when you get out of your car. You will want to toss these ahead of you, to clear your path of snakes, animals, and then as you get closer to the building, hit the side of it (not the windows). Those loud thumps will bring anyone or anything inside out to investigate. It's always better to deal with them outside than inside where you're trapped.

If there are only two of you, one stands watch, looking out while the other goes inside, but time it. The person outside must go inside in 5 minutes, no matter what the other person wants. That way, they aren't waiting there for someone to come out who is injured or unconscious. Switch off. Give each other turns to investigate.

We keep our car nearby but try to park behind if we can so no one sees we stopped there and are vulnerable and alone, but we like to be able to jump into it. Sometimes, we've had situations where one of us is in the

Abandoned Places: Abandoned Memories (Appalachian Edition)

car while the other jumps out and takes pictures of the outside of the building in scary towns known to be mostly empty and questionably being meth lab towns.

We never get out and explore in those types of towns. They let you know you're not welcome either. The locals stop in their cars when they see you photographing their store fronts. They glare at you and let you know they don't want you there.

If you go online and look up urbex (urban exploration) sites, you can find places others have explored in your area. If you look at a map of your route and see odd small town names that you aren't familiar with, look them up for population and look up Google images. When we went to West Virginia, we would type in each town we drove through and the word "abandoned" next to the town name on a Google image search. This led us to find if a town had a lot of abandoned sites or not and the types of abandoned sites.

When it comes to photographing abandoned sites, we often tell people to consider these elements –

Lighting: There is nothing more dramatic than a bit of light coming through a broken window, beams of light sparkling from holes in the roof, and some times, one strong focused shaft of light –

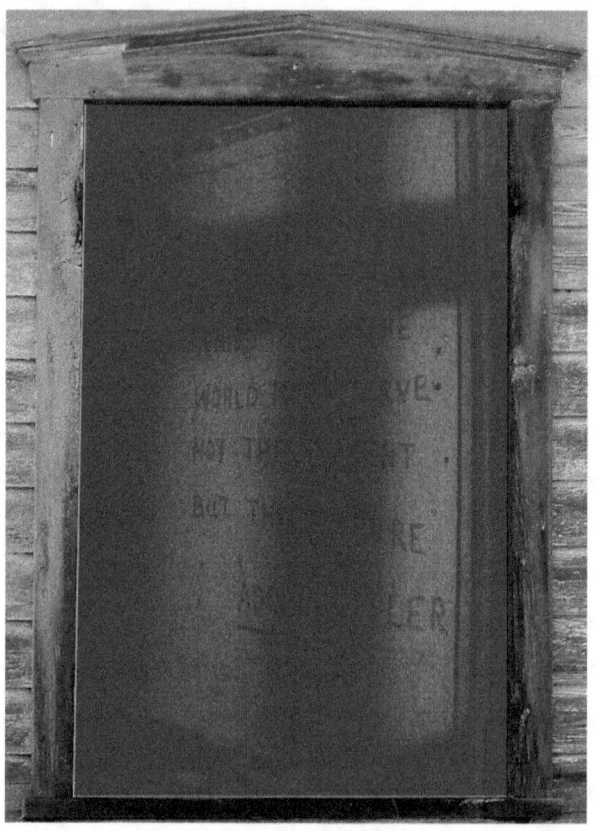

(Above-the light hit this wall in a jail where someone had posted Nazi hate words, and the bars cast a cross-shaped shadow, blotting it out)

Abandoned Places: Abandoned Memories (Appalachian Edition)

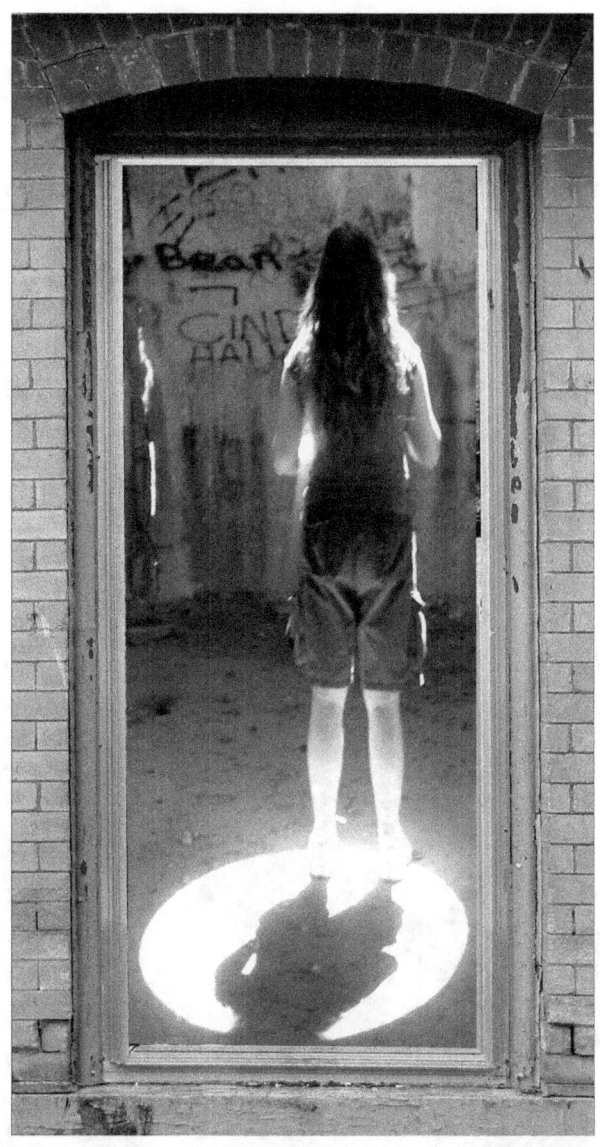

(Above-Sharon in a shaft of light coming through the ceiling, like being beamed up by a spaceship)

Abandoned Places: Abandoned Memories (Appalachian Edition)

Framing: Utilize windows to reflect what is behind the photographer to show the entire 360 degree perspective or use them to look out from darkness to the beauty outside and the contrast. Doorways, windows, cracks, and ceiling holes are all fantastic opportunities. Just remember to turn off the flash on your camera. Had I used a flash on the bars of that prison (above), I wouldn't have captured that subtle cross shape from the bars.

Found objects: The most emotionally moving photographs show what was left behind, unattended, forgotten, telling only part of a story.

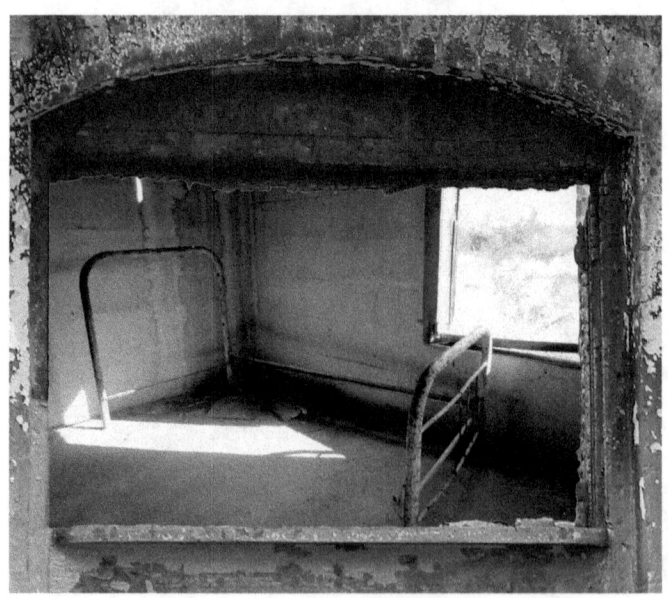

(*Above-this lone bed frame with the light hitting it makes for a very barren visual, but also the mental. One*

Abandoned Places: Abandoned Memories (Appalachian Edition)

envisions the occupant who slept in that bed, what they saw out the window, how they lived....)

Children's toys, a book left open, a recliner chair with nothing nearby – all sadly forgotten objects. In one burned out building, we found a corner shelf with the dishes still on it, but the wall nearby completely gone. You can go into a building and find intact blinds in an empty room or a chandelier still in place, the floorboards broken below. Take advantage of these lone signs of prior human habitation.

Nature's encroachment: Faded signs are one of the first indicators of nature's effects on an abandoned site.

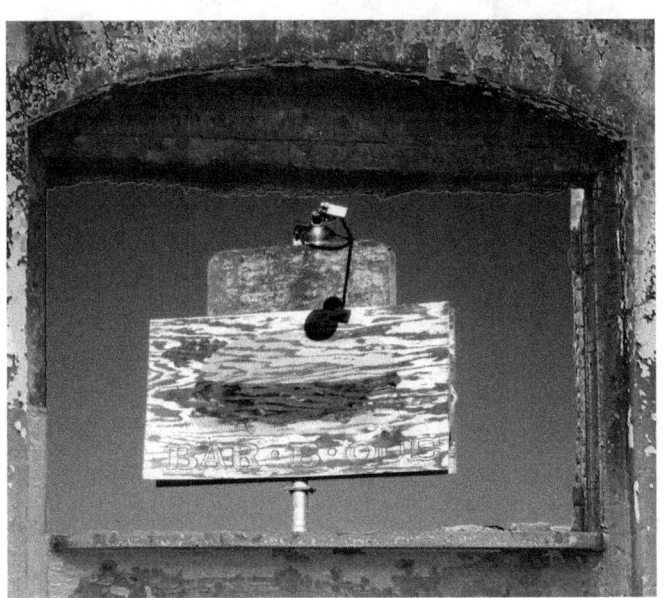

Abandoned Places: Abandoned Memories (Appalachian Edition)

What nature does to wood, metal, and glass makes for very texturally interesting photographs. And, what animals, wind, rain, snow, and sunlight do to buildings can be quite impressive. In Appalachia, we ran into a lot of vines wanting to reclaim the buildings into the landscape.

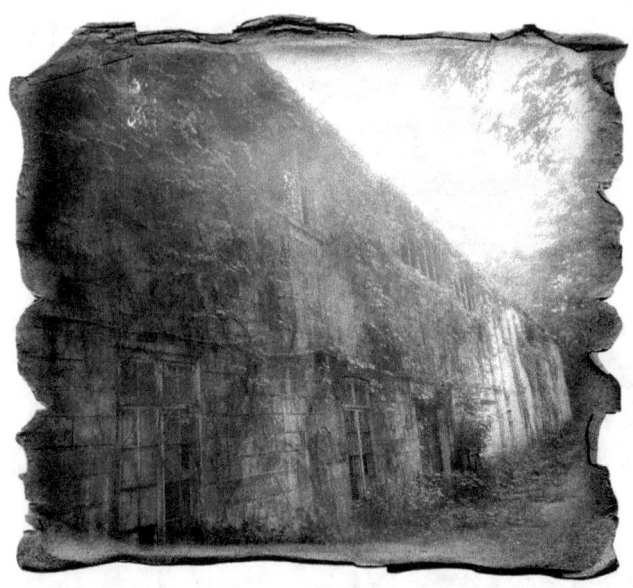

(*Above – this building was being eaten alive by vines*)

It's always a good idea to go to a favorite site in different seasons. There is nothing like seeing bare vines inside a window or snow piled up on a sill compared to the lush green tropical explosion of summertime. Rust, rotting

Abandoned Places: Abandoned Memories (Appalachian Edition)

wood, broken windows, crumbling walls – all effects of nature that age a building and make it look authentically abandoned for quite some time. Take advantage of bubbling paint from a recent fire or spider webs in windows.

Perspective/Scale: If a building is fat and short, get on your belly and take the shot to exaggerate it. If it is tall and narrow, get under it, looking up at the height of it and the peak. If it's missing a wall, get inside and look out at the missing wall instead of shooting into the building. If you go inside and it feels claustrophobic, show the funhouse effect – tilt the camera like this (below)

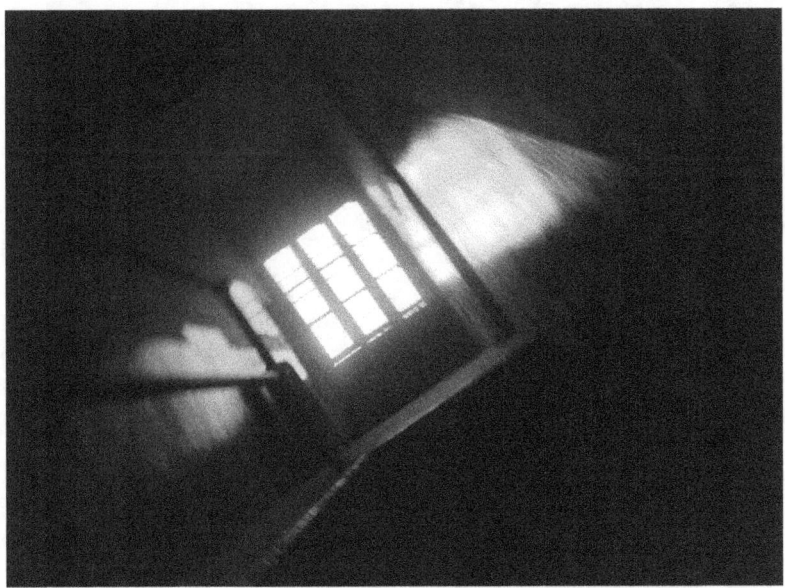

Abandoned Places: Abandoned Memories (Appalachian Edition)

Each location will speak to you with mood and lighting, disarray and sometimes disgust. Some might be tagged by teenagers with spray paint, others never opened up since they were abandoned. Utilize these aspects to tell a story. You will be amazed at the photographs you take in abandoned sites. They are vastly different than photographing people, pets or landscapes. They move you and create a longing and a fear that is inherent in all of us at the thought of being left behind.

Abandoned Places: Abandoned Memories (Appalachian Edition)

CHAPTER TWO
ABANDONED BRIDGE HOUSE

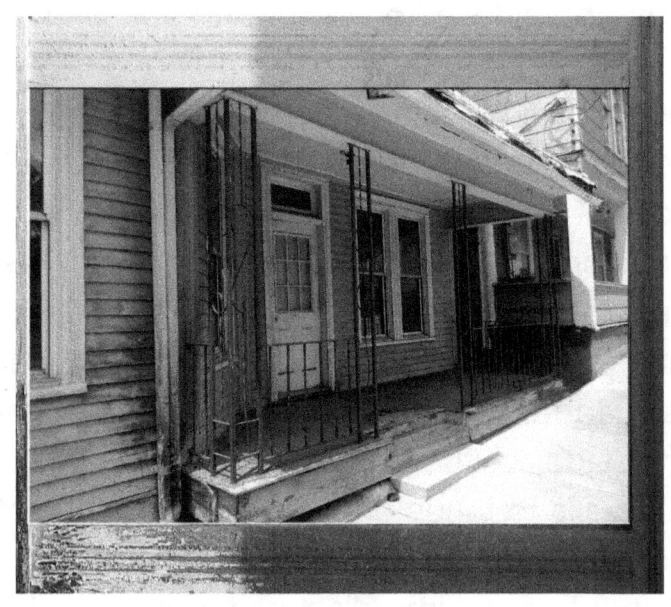

We had wandered into this quiet town in the West Virginia mountains a few times to photograph and each time we crossed the bridge, we slowed down and pointed out the charming house on the corner. It literally hugged the cliff down to the river below and appeared as if it singularly held the bridge as it entered the crowded town.

It was sunny, hot, humid day when we pulled the car over and got out to look at it up close. The faded yellow, charming little cottage home was in a very tenuous position on the hillside. It was hard to imagine that it could remain there safely for much longer.

Julie walked onto the bridge to photograph the cottage from the side. She was impressed with its charm and style and mentioned, "if I were going to live in a little town in West Virginia, this is the house I'd want."

It certainly had a positioning that made itself the ambassador of the town by being the first place to say "hello" to visitors as they drove over the New River.

Julie felt challenged by the precarious filming opportunities. The alleyway was off limits that went downhill and there was only bridge, cliff and water below on the other side, so the options were limiting. Still, she found the details to focus on to show the magic of the once adorable home.

We spent some time discussing how we'd renovate the place if we had it. The wood trim was mildewed and termite eaten. The foundation needed reinforcement from the crumbling cliff below. It seemed better to just render it to earth again, but they simply didn't make them like this one anymore.

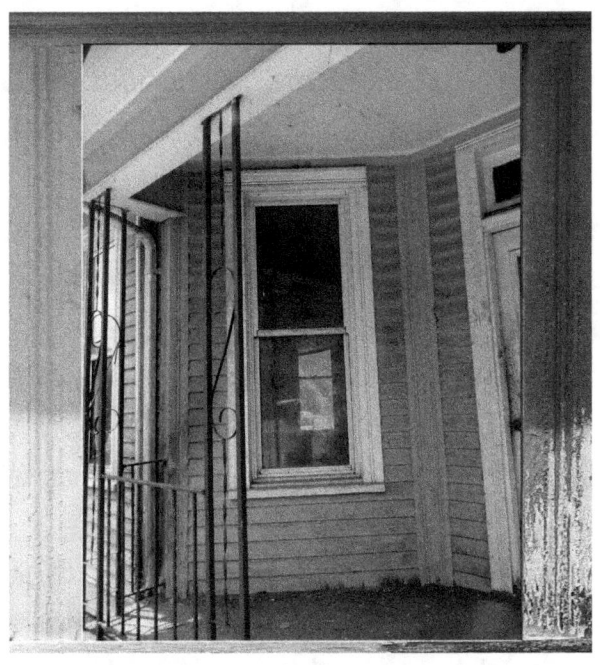

My fear of heights included walking out on the bridge. I did it to get a better view, but as always, the vertigo drove me nuts. The sight out of the corners of my eyes showed me that my stance was precarious, another reason I hated flying and being able to see out of both windows out of the corner of my eyes enough to feel vertigo.

The occasional pickup truck rolled over the bridge and into the impoverished forgotten railroad town. Not far away, drug deals and prostitution occurred in not so discrete manner on a main street. Women with lots of babies close in age, ushered their way, cigarette in hand, slouchy tank top, and flip flops into the store to get some

Abandoned Places: Abandoned Memories (Appalachian Edition)

soda pop. Such an idyllic looking town harbored a world of indifference and fixed income, drug issues, and bad choices for the young. The average age of the citizens was 62.

The charming antiquated skyline of the little hamlet above the angled roof line of the cottage made a picturesque sight. We both kept going back and forth trying to capture the quirky perched nature of the town above the water, the railroad tracks, the mountain looming dark green and forbidding in the backdrop like a silent tsunami.

I was hesitant to think I could gather much from the place, but the doorknob to the front door, even though something no doubt touched by many, I knew that this antique would hold within it the memories of one person who touched it the most. Unlike a plastic doorknob or a cheap aluminum one, this heavy solid knob would be a great retainer of information.

The difficult part would be gathering information from the actual owner of the home versus someone who had touched it randomly. Sometimes, the person who held an object the longest would come through and other times, it could be the most recent person to touch it. I had yet to figure out the rhyme or reason in how the retention of information worked.

The woman who touched the doorknob in the past struck me quite easily and I envisioned her, the way she carried herself, her introverted nature and self consciousness, and the grief held tightly within. This was going to be a powerful read....

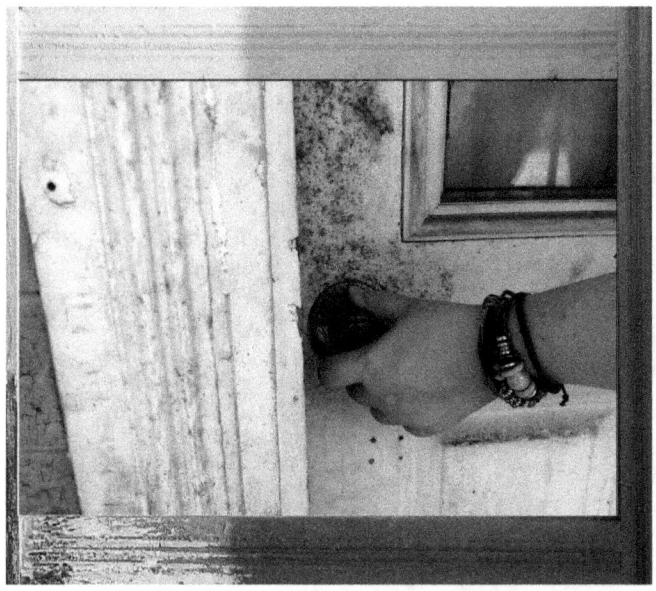

Abandoned Places: Abandoned Memories (Appalachian Edition)

POTLUCKS AND BIBLES

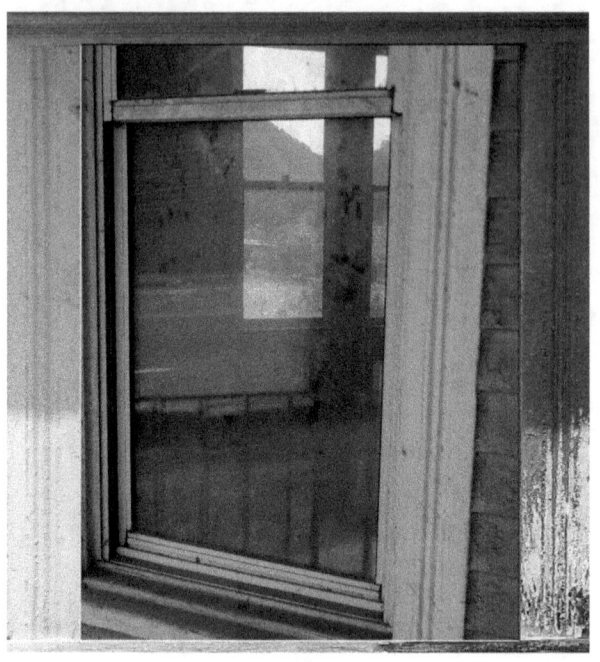

If one more person knocked at her door, she wasn't going to arrive with a smile while her feet tortured her. The table was already laden with roast beef, casseroles, enchiladas, cornbread, and more food than any 105 pound woman could eat in a century. And, it wasn't as if someone in grief wanted to eat. If they wanted to leave something useful, they'd allow her to borrow a handy husband to fix the leaking sink and roof.

Abandoned Places: Abandoned Memories (Appalachian Edition)

She sighed with the realization that the disarray since her husband's long-term illness was only going to grow worse. He never allowed her to so much as hold a hammer in her hand, so how would she upkeep their charming cottage in its former glory?

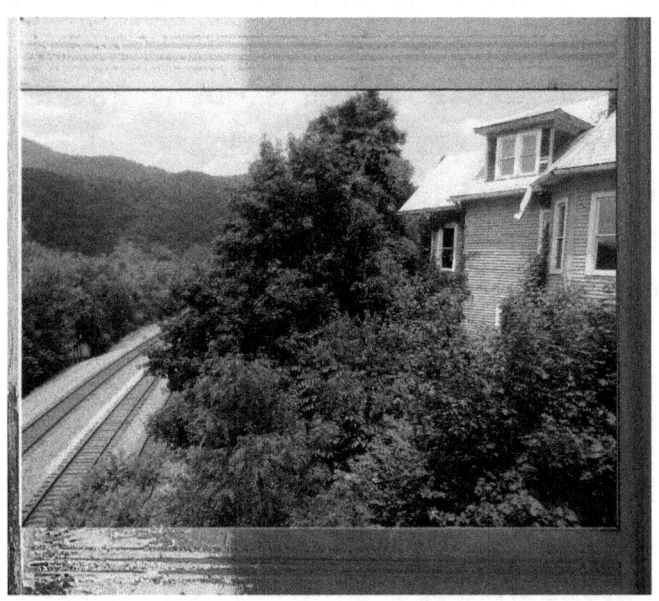

The new dress shoes in practical black were pinching her toes and cutting a slice in the back of each heel. She could feel the cold sticky beads of blood moistening the virgin leather.

She wore her good brown leathers to church on Sunday and sometimes the white patent leather ones in the summertime, but neither seemed appropriate for the funeral and her peers let her know that he would have

Abandoned Places: Abandoned Memories (Appalachian Edition)

wanted her to at least be appropriate for the occasion. She only wore pastels since she was a child. Happy colors promised happy things.

Her arthritic fingers plucked at the black sheer ruffles on her dress and then she recalled that her friend buttoned her up the back. She was now locked into the depressing shroud.

With no doubts in her mind that he awaited her in Heaven and want her to continue on, she kicked off her shoes with a groan. The physical pain helped her to focus on something other than the silent home that had once been their quiet retreat.

There were no petunias in pots this spring. She had been at the hospital nearly every day. He came home for weeks at a time before having to go back. The summer was long and hot, miserable and over a time of accepting his impending death with each visit to the medical center, she was more than prepared when he moved on the Lord's side.

Most wives would wail and rattle against the fates, but her faith kept her focused on his purpose which was not of this Earth, but in Heaven. She would join him in time, but for now she must decide how to get out of the dress that felt every minute as if it were tightening and choking the breath from her.

She picked up her sewing scissors and cut the hem of the dress. It was costly compared to her usual clothing, but to be respectful in the funeral ceremony, it was a small cost. It wasn't like she intended to ever wear it again and she certainly didn't want a friend burying her some day in the nasty color. Still, the sound of rendering fabric made her cringe, but the desire to be rid of it was so strong that she took the half cut fabric and pulled it in two directions at once, feeling the chill autumn air hitting her flesh as she shimmied out of the dangling panels.

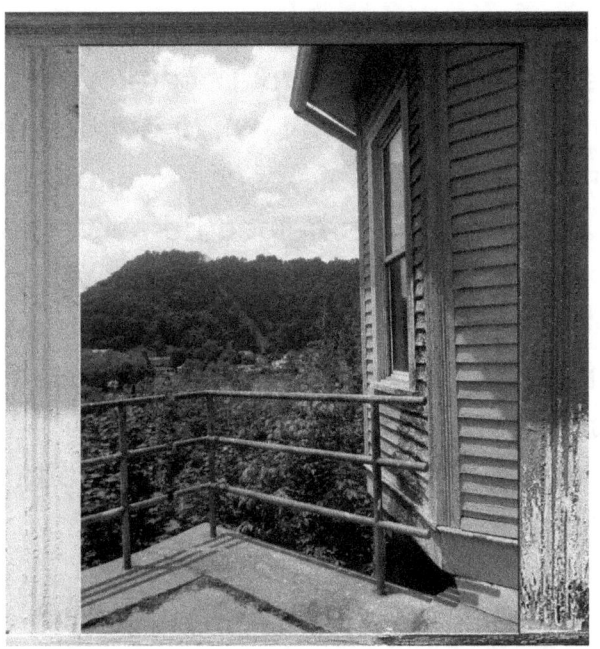

A knock at the door startled her and she clutched the fabric to her chest. Deep in the dark recesses of their bedroom, no one could see her from the front door, but the thought brought a blush to her cheeks. She pulled on her house dress and looked around for her slippers, opting to go barefoot to answer it, though it galled her to have anyone see her naked feet.

Cracking the door open, the fading light outside made it hard to make out the dark figure, but by the girth of it and the height, it was her dearest friend. Allowing Mary to see her out of her mourning dress so soon after her husband's funeral, she opened the door and let her in.

"I have two more casseroles in my fridge, but honestly, I have no idea how you'd finish them. I haven't seen you eat more than a couple of crackers." Mary tsked as she pushed aside a warm bowl of potato salad and plucked her hand into a plate of cookies to bring one up to her mouth. As always, she helped herself to some milk from the icebox and sat down at the recliner chair and relaxed. She was out of her funeral clothing and into her usual moo-moo shaped dress and flat moccasins.

"Sit, sit." Mary gestured.

She sank down into the worn sofa, certain that her weary body may never get up again.

"It was an impressive turnout."

She nodded.

"I do believe Ted was considering you. I think you might have a suitor already."

She shook her head. The last thing she needed was another man underfoot. Not that she didn't love her husband, but it was not an active love. It was a comfortable and companionable one. The concepts of courting and romance were half a century behind her.

"I was not at all amazed that Ima wore that yellow dress. A yellow dress to a funeral! And, she brought a date. Who was that man? He's not from here." Mary finished chewing.

The easy thing about being with Mary is that she never expected conversation from her. She was not the chatty type except when she had public appearances at church or the store. Then, she knew how to make small talk enough to not look painfully shy. But, she was, and exquisitely so.

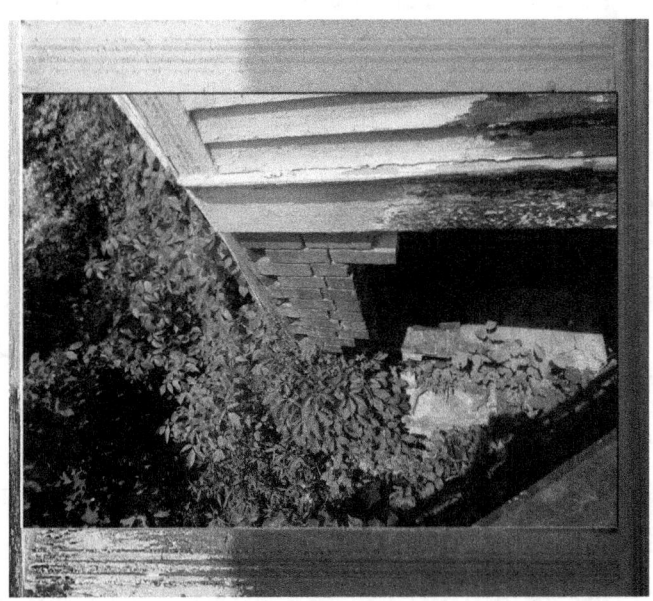

Abandoned Places: Abandoned Memories (Appalachian Edition)

"Someone asked if you were putting your place up for sale. The gall! Who was that? Oh yes, it was Burt. He wouldn't buy your place, he doesn't sell real estate. Why he cares, I don't know."

"He's the executor of the estate."

Mary raised a brow. "I had no idea that they still spoke. I thought once Burt moved to the city, the brothers quit speaking. You would have been just fine to handle the estate."

She yawned. "No, I didn't want to deal with those details. I never handled the finances."

"The Reverend said something about Wednesday's potluck and I had to laugh. I said that maybe you should bring all the foods."

That made her laugh with a snort of unwelcome humor, but it was true. What was she to do with all the food? Having the families just remake their usual dishes again seemed wasteful.

Mary chuckled. "The lasagna and pork and beans casserole will do nicely. I'll come by and help you. You are going, aren't you?"

Mary studied her as if noticing for the first time that there were no tears. Not the entire day. Not even when the choir sang "Amazing Grace," his favorite song. Not even when his best friend stood up and told stories of their youth. And, not even when the minister pressed his

Abandoned Places: Abandoned Memories (Appalachian Edition)

hand to hers and studied her with those knowing gray eyes filled with empathy.

"I'll be there." She yawned again.

"Okay, dear. I do believe it's time for me to get going and let you get some rest. Do you need anything?"

She got up and ushered her friend gladly to the door.

"I'm fine. Just need a good sleep. I'll have few bites of your cornbread before I tuck myself in."

Mary hugged her with that big warm bear hug that she had become used to tolerating. Her own family was not affectionate in the least and hugging and expressions of uncontrolled fondness were all so awkward, especially on a person who was as tiny and timid as she.

This time, though, she felt the extra squeeze of reassurance and she responded with one of her own. Mary must have noticed the tone of her embrace. She stepped back and smiled.

"You'll be just fine."

She nodded.

When the door closed, she let out a breath, as every bone in her body rattled into a settled position of defeat. There was no more posing. No more concerning herself with others opinions or judgments. There was just her, telling the world to go away by turning out the porch light and locking the deadbolts. It was yet another nightly ritual she had taken over since her husband turned ill, something she had never had to think about in all their time living there.

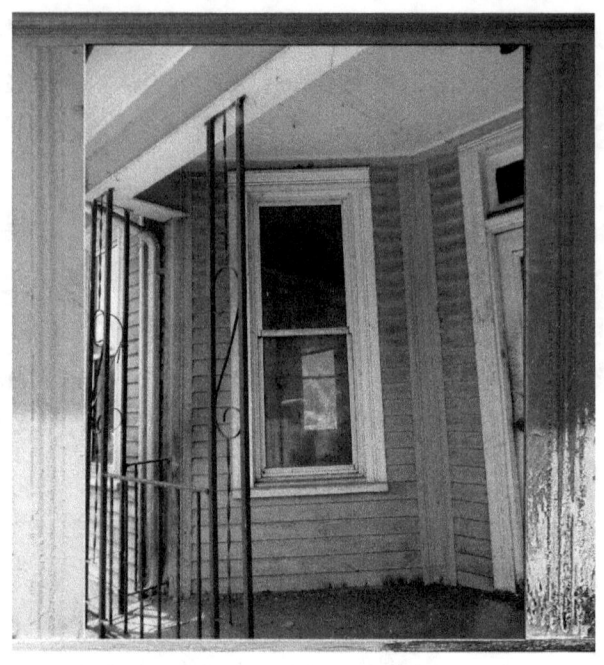

Defeated, she shuffled back to their bedroom. *Her* bedroom and faced the lonely bed. At some point she would have to sleep in it again, perhaps in the center of it where she never was able to sleep. But, for now, the sofa beckoned her, as lumpy and miserable as it was, it offered her the sound of the TV so she felt less alone, and no feeling of missing a limb like sleeping in their bed without him beside her offered.

Once she sank her weary body into the sofa, pulled up the warm frayed blanket they used to put over their laps when they watched TV, she set the channel for the simple soothing voices of the Christian channel and rested her heavy head against the flattened pillow, turned onto her side, closed her eyes, sighed out loud, and felt the hot roll of a tear from the corner of her eye.

Her body quivered in fear of the unknown, the future, the loneliness, the void before her; as the pillow slowly soaked and an audible sound escaped for the first time, followed by heart-wrenching sobs with no barriers to the floodgates they opened.

BONUS
PSYCHOMETRY SKILLS

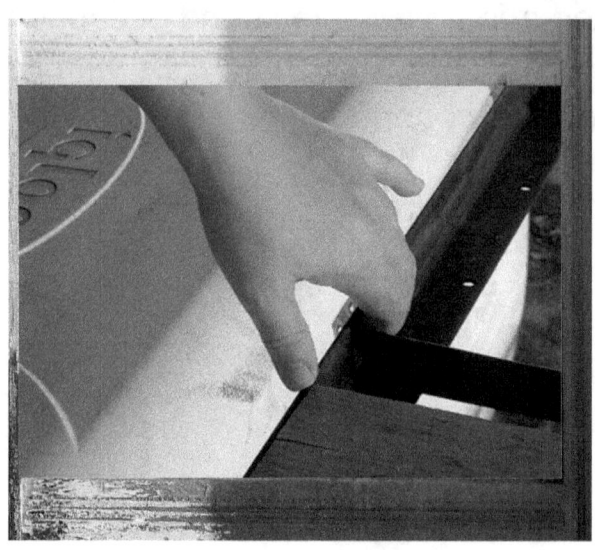

What is it like to touch an object and get information, other than texture, weight, temperature and shape?

Having the ability all my life, it's not an easy one to describe. It goes something like this; I touch the object, there is a transfer of information by some means that allows me to know if it has positive or negative energy in

Abandoned Places: Abandoned Memories (Appalachian Edition)

its contained memories, male/female, mood/tone, and then more in depth images, names, surroundings, situations and associations. It's like tapping into someone's memories and it's out of context. You don't know who they are, where you are, or what you're picking up. If someone dropped into my high school prom memories, they would have images of a loud band, a swimming pool, my feelings about my date, my attitude about the event. It would be very disorienting.

There are many guidelines for refining psychometry skills. I begin with showing a person how to know the hand they read with. We generally have a hand that takes in energy and information and one that puts it out from us to others. More often than not, that hand that reads things or takes them in is the opposite hand of what you write with, but that isn't always the case, so I suggest a little test.

Abandoned Places: Abandoned Memories (Appalachian Edition)

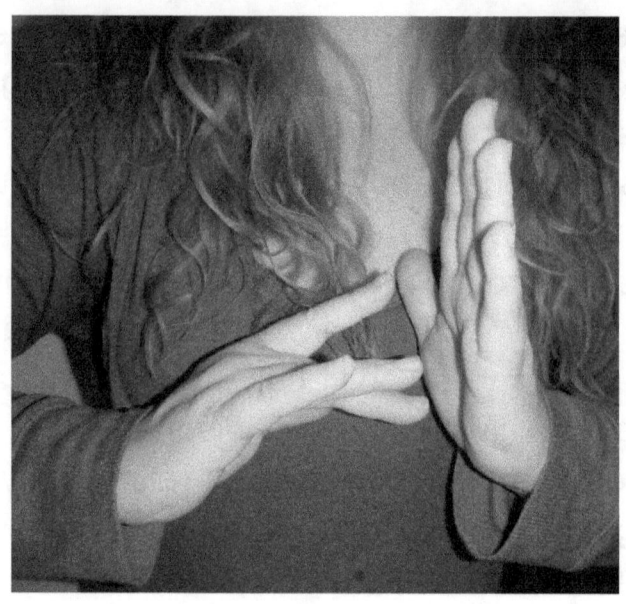

Test: Hold your hands up in front of your chest, palms facing each other. Put them far apart enough that if you bend the fingers on one hand, they don't touch the other hand, but they *almost do*. Now, take your right hand and stroke the fingers towards the left palm. Do you feel anything in the left palm? Now, reverse and stroke with the left hand toward the right palm. Do you feel anything in your right palm? The hand that feels the tickling strokes is your "reading/receiving" (energy in) hand, the hand that was stroking is your "sending/healing" (energy out) hand.

Use your reading/receiving hand whenever you want to read an object, touch someone and see if they are either genuine or to feel their pain. Use your sending/healing hand whenever you either want to

Abandoned Places: Abandoned Memories (Appalachian Edition)

intimidate and control/calm someone or give them your energy to heal them.

If you would like to try your hand at reading an object, just remember that you cannot let the visual of the object distract you in any way. A woman gave me a beautiful necklace that looked quite expensive. I, however, picked up on her and a group of friends at a Vegas weekend and a claw machine filled with jewelry. In fact, she had been on a girl's getaway weekend to Vegas and the necklace was her winning in a claw machine. Had I let my intellect get in the way, I would have missed a dead-on read.

When you read an object, don't think "this is a ring" or "this is a key." The object means nothing in the read, it's the information it holds psychically. Don't think of the context of a key's use or a ring's use. Just let emotions, images, and everything to spill out. Say it out loud to a notetaker or write it down, but get it out without trying to interpret its meaning.

Eventually, you can tie the bits together into a story that ties together all those elements. That is more advanced, like shooting 3-point baskets. You need lots of practice. And, a reader is only as good as her knowledge in general. If you have never been exposed to the Jewish culture and you pick up something in the reading that makes no sense, you may dismiss it. However, if you know how Hebrew tradition treats death, suddenly the word "shiva" has a frame of reference and is not nonsensical and you can further the read.

For my whole life, whenever I read someone who was indigenous, they were difficult to separate. I could mix up a Asian with a Hebrew person or an African with an Inuit. It took me years to find a way to differentiate them in my mind by focusing on the spiritual sense from the groups so I would better be able to determine which ethnicity I was reading.

It isn't always easy to go deeper and deeper. Sometimes, you might just get a "good" or "bad" vibe from it or a "male" or "female" impression. It's vital to ask the person whose item you're reading to say nothing. Turn away from them. Do not look at them. Simply rattle off everything you get. They will make sense of it later. If you look to them for hints of right or wrong, you will be led down a dead end path. The ego wants to provide more and more when you know you made a "hit." When you visually begin to scan the other person's expressions, you alter your read. And, it corrupts the whole process.

The three enemies of psychometry reads are; interpretation, ego and intellect.

I once read someone and was dead on accurate, but I assumed he was the elder child because he was responsible. I was correct that he was the responsible child, but he was actually the younger child. Our knowledge and frame of reference alter interpretation. Had I just said, "you were the responsible child," I would have been 100% accurate, but by going a step further and "assuming" he was the elder, my scoring was much weaker.

Ego is another big roadblock. We want to give accurate reads and we can easily be distracted by response from those we are reading. If we do well, we can also get cocky and give more info when we don't really have more. We are now picking extemporaneous information and have left the main path by pushing too hard. How often do you see psychics on TV give a reading and then go off on a tangent and the client's face goes blank? They blame it often times on picking up "someone else" but they have tried to give more, more, more and they have reached the point of no return.

Intellect gets in our way because we look at an object and think we understand much just from its age, value, care, prestige, and we also think of its function and the context in which it was used. As well, we look at the person we are reading for and make assumptions about class, lifestyle, and other key clues. We must always treat an object and the person we are reading for as if we have no clue what they are or how they have lived or been used.

Abandoned Places: Abandoned Memories (Appalachian Edition)

Like any skill, psychometry takes regular work. You have to build it just like your ability to shoot a 3-point basket . You come to know what you feel in your mind and body when you make an accurate "hit." In fact, I tell people to test daily online at a psychic testing site just to learn that feeling of "sureness" that comes when you were correct. I like to use www.gotpsi.org

Abandoned Places: Abandoned Memories (Appalachian Edition)

CHAPTER THREE
ABANDONED STORE

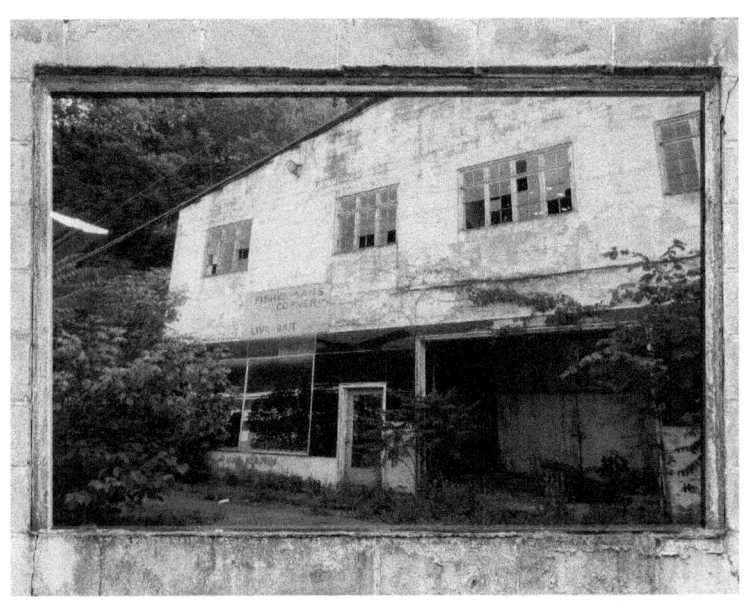

I remembered getting candy at this store as a kid when we came to West Virginia to visit relatives. The large two-story building was a classic with the old-fashioned Coke icebox and shelves of a wild mix of candy and fishing lures, sundries and dried jerky.

Julie stood outside the structure and studied the long-abandoned site with wonder and curiosity. Peering inside the front area of the store, old display cases sat with bushes and young trees growing through and around them.

"This is amazing." Julie remarked. "Look at that Coke refrigerator. It's probably worth serious cash. I can't believe they left it." She turned to me. "How long has this been abandoned?"

If the broken windows and almost completely obliterated sign painted onto the building's brick didn't give it away, the rapid heavy weight of decades of vines showed the reality.

"I photographed it in 2005, eight year ago, and it was long abandoned then. In fact, it looks a helluva lot like it did then." I walked along the side of the building where rows of windows exposed the interior.

Abandoned Places: Abandoned Memories (Appalachian Edition)

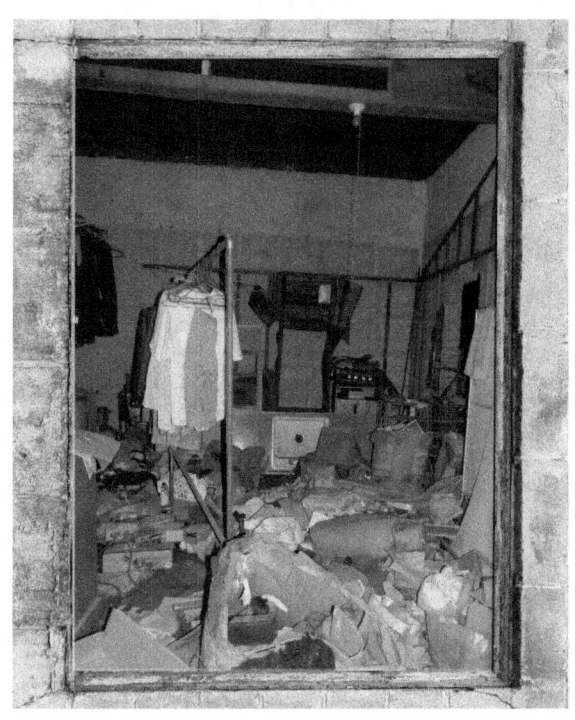

Leaning forward and gazing in, my eyes adjusting to the darkness, I viewed the same clothing racks and boxes, toys and other items that I had photographed so long ago. The mildew wet smell from within mixed with the fresh lush green of early summer outside and my stomach flip flopped. It was time for lunch, but I was glad we were poking around before we ate. The nastiness of the abandoned gutted insides and years of decay would have caused bile to rise in my throat.

Julie rounded the corner and stopped to get some shots of the massive wall and the almost total engorgement of vines upon its aged surface. She stopped and peered into a room through a broken window.

"It's amazing how much they left behind."

"My sister told me that indigents would sleep in here during rough seasons. See the makeshift bedding?" I pointed to an area near a wall where blankets and clothing and pillows were stacked up next to ice chest. "I can't be sure," I added, "but I do think that when I compare the previous pictures, nothing has changed."

"That's amazing!" Julie exclaimed. "It's right here on a fairly main road with broken windows and no one messed with it?"

I nodded. "This is not the kind of town that would be fascinated with an abandoned building. They're common and most folks think they're a blight and pretend they aren't part of the landscape."

She shook her head and moved on to get new angles with her camera while I contemplated how amazingly similar it was to eight years previously. The entire town, as I knew it, had changed only a tiny fraction from when I was a child decades ago. Other than a store name changing or the addition of a McDonald's, there were no effects of the passage of time. Even the ever-flowing river that the town was based upon, had not worn down its banks by any notable difference.

Julie wandered up and down the structure, taking it in, noting details about the windows, the sign, the

Abandoned Places: Abandoned Memories (Appalachian Edition)

proportions, and the dark voids of broken windows cram-packed with vines looking for a hold to continue their invasion of the undisturbed mass. The sun slanted in at a good angle and Julie squatted down to take advantage of what it did to the bits of glass still remaining.

I considered the people who had found refuge in the mildewed interior in the icy elements of the mountains of Appalachia, seeking warmth buried under layers of discarded clothing and rags. I shivered. Railroad and mining towns that the entire state was based upon were dwindling. The only remaining occupants were the retirees who lived there many generations and refused to start new.

My mother had worked hard to join the effort to stop strip mining, but the natural beauty of the state was scarred and it didn't miss my notice that some towns, like the one that my family lived in, the population with cancer was astronomically high. All the natural resources of West Virginia were squeezed dry for profit and left the miners crippled, the buildings barren, and the waterways corrupt.

Something about the old building; probably filled with mold, bugs, asbestos and mildew made me shiver and step back with repugnance. Spiders dangled from webs in the windows, vines gripped the sills, pulling them loose from their mooring, and cars drove past, the drivers not even casting a single glance at the forgotten site.

Abandoned Places: Abandoned Memories (Appalachian Edition)

It was time to get a read, but I had no idea what I was in for when I reached out to touch the building....

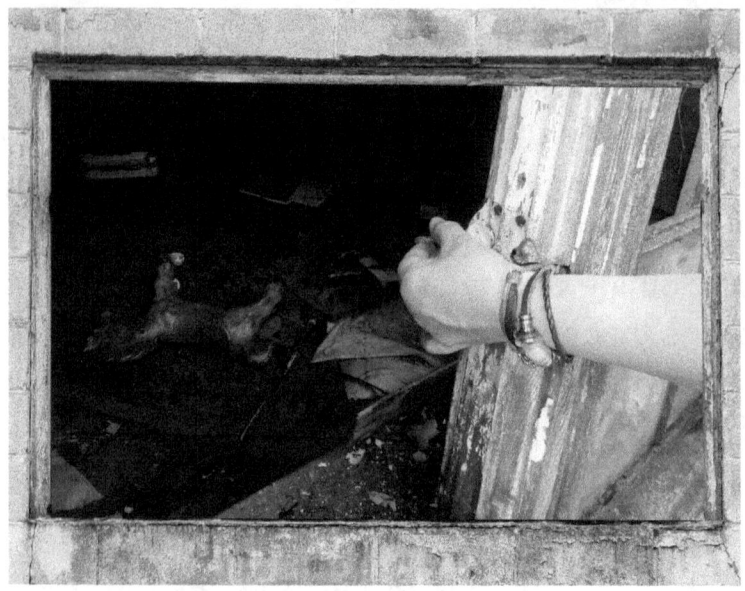

CRANKED UP

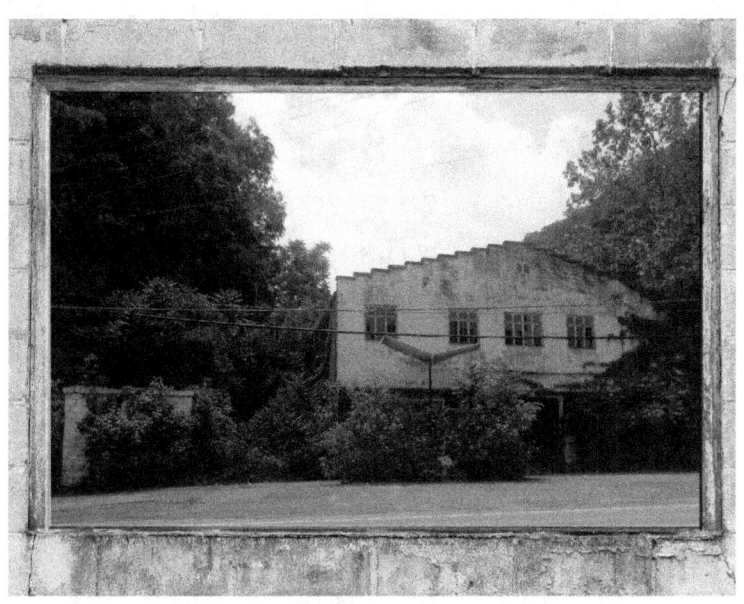

He didn't do his business in town. Everyone saw him loitering on the corner, so he moved it onto the road. In his brother-in-law's truck he tore up the roadway, up and down the mountains and riverside, to make deals where he could find them. Sometimes, folks were accommodating and, other times they fucking pissed him off.

"Crank! Crank!"

Abandoned Places: Abandoned Memories (Appalachian Edition)

At the sound of Bud's voice, he swung around to hush the big simple-minded lookout. He shoved him back behind the abandoned building.

"Don't call me that!"

"Ever'one calls you Crank." The man shuffled, hands in his pockets while the wiry small man waved a fist at him.

"Don't call me nothin'!" He spat and shoved past the hired goon and into the darkened room that smelled of mildew mixed with leftover discarded food cartons from previous homeless people who sought shelter in there on rainy nights. He shuddered, vaguely recalling a drug-induced night on the floor with a rat nibbling on his sock and flinging it against the wall as he shook from its hold.

His ever-dilated pupils had no adjusting to do as he walked over a pile of clothing and broken boards towards the well-dressed man leaning against the wall smoking a cigarette.

"Whadaya have today?"

"Thirty tablets." Crank reached into his flannel shirt pocket and extracted a prescription bottle, holding it up in the air. "Just filled."

"Vicodin?"

"Oxycontin."

"Bless you Jesus!" Mr. Suit hooted. "Ya didn't bring me more weed again. Got anyone else gettin' a cut of

Abandoned Places: Abandoned Memories (Appalachian Edition)

this?" It was normal to have someone selling their pain pills for some cash.

Crank shook his head. "Slipped in and sneaked it off the dresser."

The man's chuckle turned into a chronic miner's cough.

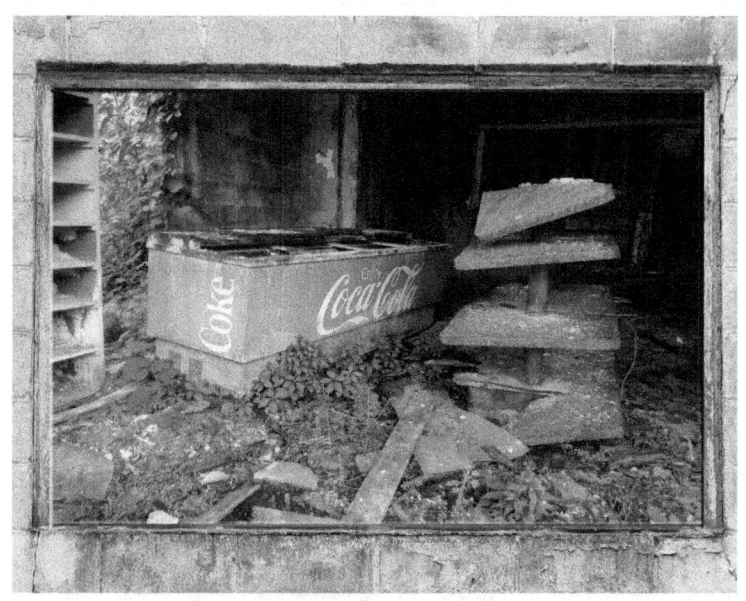

Crank waited, feeling antsy and distracted as always. He'd been off meth for eight weeks, but that didn't stop him from looking for anything that might crank him back up. Three energy drinks with Ritalin had him feeling the twitches. Soon, it would give way to higher and higher anxiety, followed by the damn crash that made him feel like he had some kind of chronic illness. He shoved his hands deeper into his pockets and paced.

The cough turned back into a laugh.

"You never change." The man wheezed. "You're too fuckin' old for speed. You should take to rotgut like your daddy did and pickle yourself, you stupid bastard."

Crank's temples throbbed, his neck muscles contracted, and his hands came out of his pockets.

"Ya want yer money?" Mr. Suit waved the bills, stopping Crank from his speedy temper.

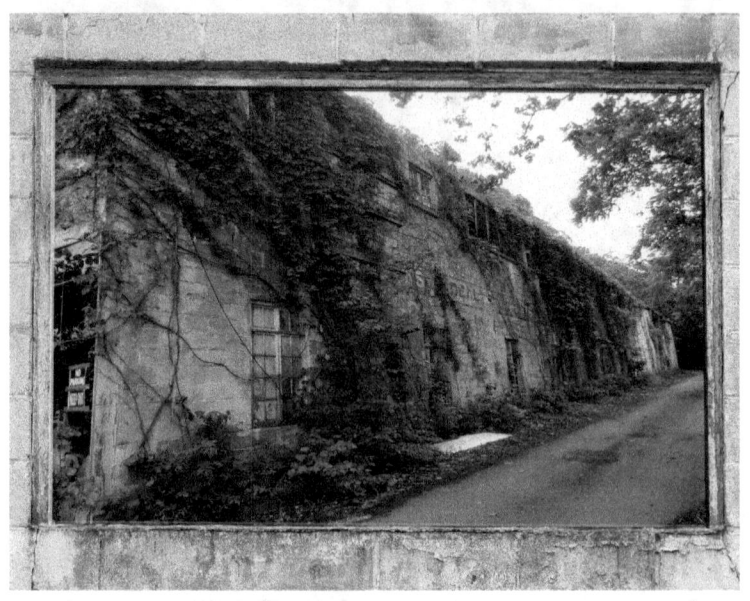

"What's this?" He flipped through the bills. "That was thirty pills." Nostrils flaring, heart thumping wildly erratic, he rushed the man whose name he never did get.

Abandoned Places: Abandoned Memories (Appalachian Edition)

The glint of a knife slipped from Mr. Suit's coat pocket. Crank felt the village idiot move up behind him, casting a deeper shadow in the already dark damp room.

"That's what it's worth."

"This ain't Vicodin. It's Oxycontin, ya fucker!" Crank growled and tossed the money at Mr. Suit and shoved the bottle of pills back into his pocket. "Ya know what they're worth. I expect fifty more than that." He waited for the expressionless man to make a decision and then shoved past his silent sentinel.

"I don't need this horseshit! I got guys in Beckley that'd buy it straight from me."

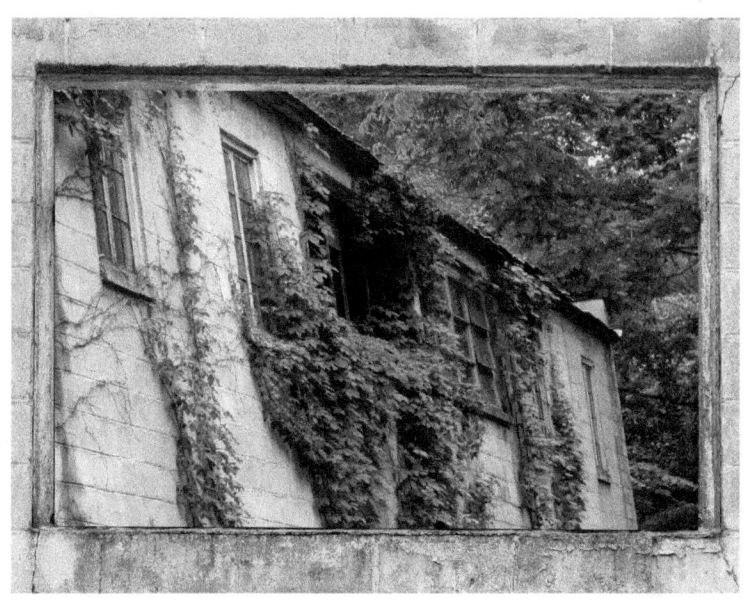

Abandoned Places: Abandoned Memories (Appalachian Edition)

"But you don't have the gas money, do ya?" The man called out as he lit another cigarette and coughed briefly. "Tell ya what, I might be able to sell them with enough profit to offer you twenty more, but this is the last time I pay so high. No one in this county can pay for `em. I gotta go in to Roanoke."

"Fuck!" Crank spat. He wanted out of there before he crashed and he wanted the cash. If he drove to Beckley, he might as well just piss the extra cash away and by the time he got there and found someone to buy, given that he'd burned his bridges with his old connections when he did meth, he'd have to crash there for the night.

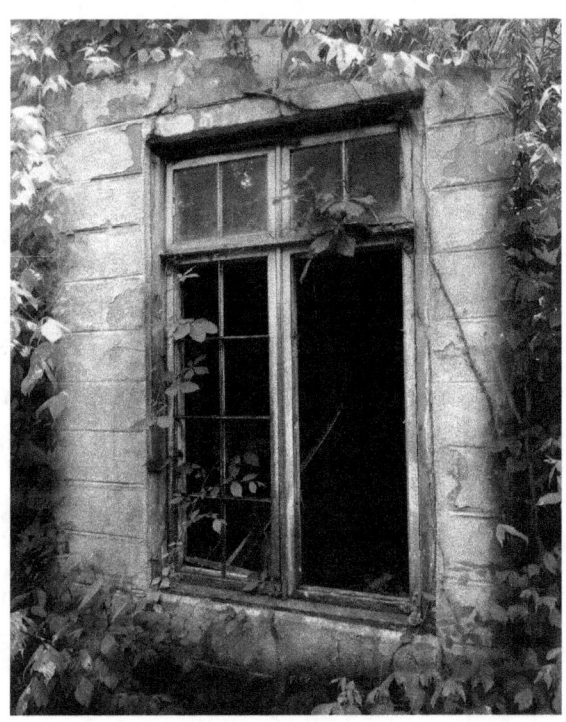

And, then, there was a warrant for his arrest for beating the shit out of that college boy who tried to jip him on a deal. That town didn't like him and, like many other towns, he'd burned his bridges and relegated himself to his hometown where there were all of a tiny handful of young cops just out of high school that didn't mind pretending they didn't see shit.

He took the cash, threw the bottle at Mr. Suit and stormed his way out of the putrid building and into the bright green outdoors.

And, just his luck, one of his ex's slowed down her car and flicked her cigarette out at him. He gave her the

Abandoned Places: Abandoned Memories (Appalachian Edition)

finger, but she was already speeding down the roadway.

Crank reached into his pocket felt around. No cigarettes. No drugs. Nothing to fucking help him as his hands shook and his teeth rattled against each other. He stormed across the street to the Dairy Queen and ordered lots of sugar. If he stayed long enough, he'd surely run into one of his high school connections. They spent their afternoons in there pimping in front of the flat-chested girls who worked the counters and giggled so much he wanted to punch their pearly white teeth in.

As he dug into the chocolate shake, a freaking cop came into the place and smiled at the girls who twittered at the counter. He got up and headed out the side door and towards the river, hoping they didn't notice his movement and decide to tap his pockets and find all the cash.

As if to top off a totally wasted day, the clouds lying low over the valley opened up a cold, heavy rain and there was no cover in sight. Either he retreated back into the Dairy Queen with the cop that had a hard-on for teens or head back to the fucking abandoned shop across the street. Like a rat with a routine, he headed back to the mildewed and musty shop once again to hide in the shadows, shivering, wet, and without any dope.

"Fuck it all!" He spat.

Like always, he was back where he started.

Abandoned Places: Abandoned Memories (Appalachian Edition)

BONUS
APPALACHIA

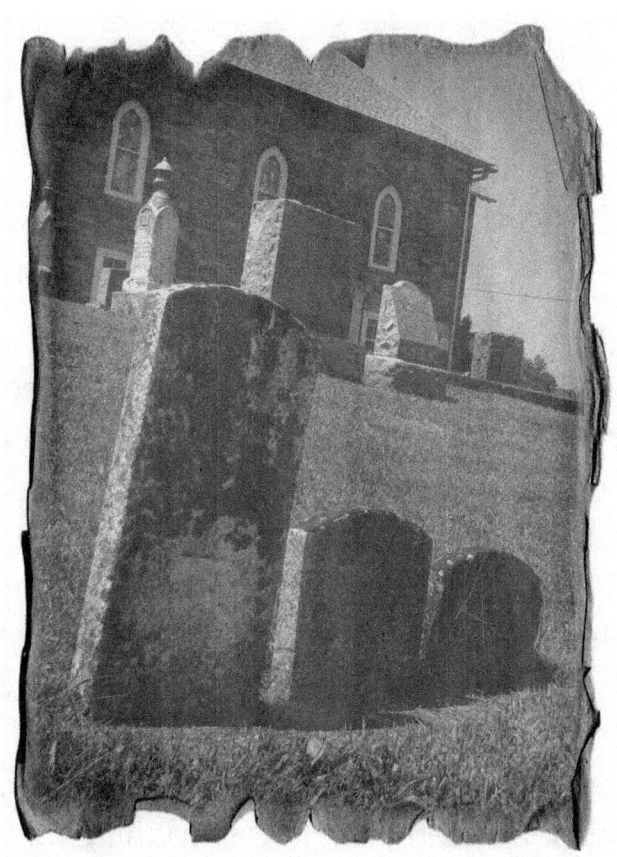

Abandoned Places: Abandoned Memories (Appalachian Edition)

The region of Appalachia is a large swath from Mississippi all the way to New York.

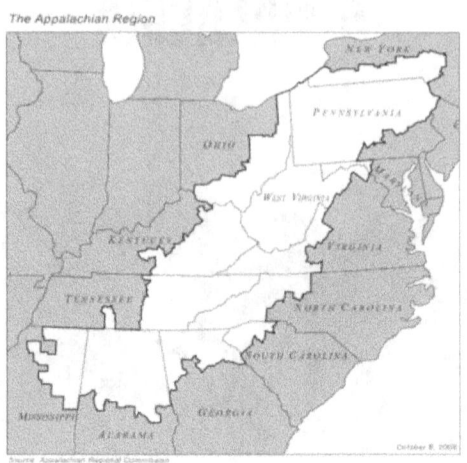

This is some of the most beautiful, geologically rich, lush, and mountainous regions in the US. It has long been mined and small towns in the more remote areas were formed to support the industry, but much of it has become abandoned during bad economic times and closure of mines and less reliance on railroads. What is left is some of the most beautiful and quaint buildings and towns struggling to remain intact.

Interestingly, the Appalachian Trail is some of the most Bigfoot-populated area in the country. Civil War history also left its mark with battlefields and ghosts. Throw into the mix the Mothman and you have a very mystical place.

Abandoned Places: Abandoned Memories (Appalachian Edition)

The culture, the people, the values of the citizens in Appalachia are the perfect example of America's founding intentions – to appreciate your origins, like Celtic songs turned to Bluegrass and made America's own. The influences of the Germans, Scots, Brits, and Irish in this region are seen in the cooking and the crafts.

Much of Appalachia is relatively poor and many towns based on mining and railroads have folded with the average age of citizens rising as youth leave the area for jobs. Because of the geological obstacles of mountains and waterways, much of it isn't a throughway like the flatland east of it. This relative "remoteness" for this part of the country also helps it to retain much of its charm, dialects, and culture.

The scenic beauty, untouched nature, historic sites and battlefields, also make Appalachia a fantastic getaway and beloved escape. Fishing, hunting and rafting are among some of the favorite activities for visitors, as well as leaf watching in the autumn along the mountain drives.

The region covers 205,000 square miles and has 25 million residents. With a great deal of natural resources and more land per person, it is a region of the country that is ideal for self sufficiency and the people who live in this paradise know how to grow and can their own foods, cut wood, and build dwellings; skills lost to many in the crowded urban centers of America. The skills that are

Abandoned Places: Abandoned Memories (Appalachian Edition)

retained by these independent people are some of the best examples of American folk art, music, food, and quilting.

The people are warm, gracious, faithful, and hard working. They are family-oriented, proud, artistic, and appreciate great longevity. The Appalachian region of America might be the last ideal microcosm of the basis for our country; resources, faith, hard work, ingenuity, and ability to work together in any conditions.

If you have never been to this region, you really must go and appreciate this slice of American, the nature, the pride, and the gracious hospitality.

CHAPTER FOUR
ABANDONED CHURCH

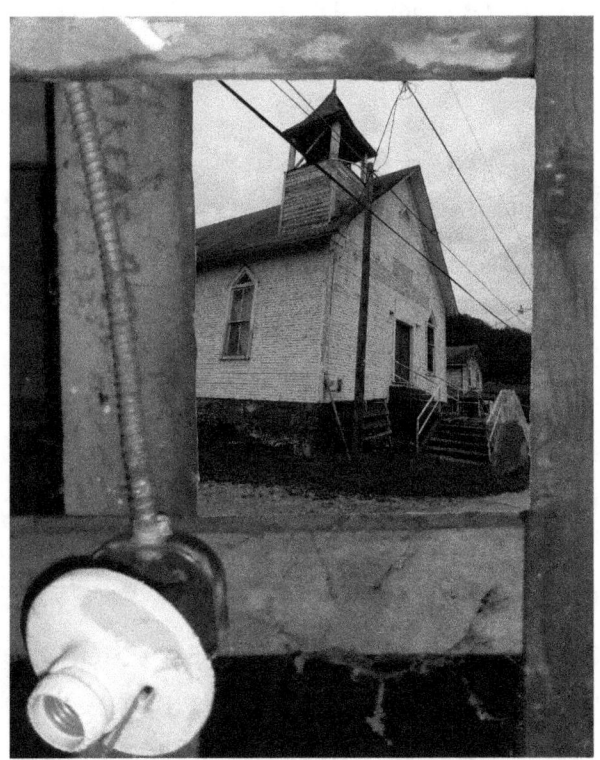

Abandoned Places: Abandoned Memories (Appalachian Edition)

We were headed through the State of West Virginia when a sign caught Sharon's eye.

"Sharon! There's a city called Sharon! We must take the exit!"

Laughing, Julie pulled the car off to the nondescript little burg where a few clapboard houses lined a main corridor and no real industry was apparent.

As Julie turned the car up the hillside, I looked up to see a white steeple. I have always had an obsession with white clapboard steeple churches with church bells. Being from the East Coast, I was used to such landmarks as a child.

"We have to photograph that!" I pointed up the hill. I had talked about us doing a church in the book if we could find an abandoned one since churches are all over Appalachia like gas stations in a city. We hadn't been lucky enough to get access to an abandoned church up close and I held little hope that we would.

Ironically, as we pulled up, a man on a ladder was removing the letters from the sign. When asked about the old church, he mentioned it was being torn down in a week.

Julie and I exchanged glances in that silent language we share when we come across something lucky and can't jump up and down like children at that moment.

Abandoned Places: Abandoned Memories (Appalachian Edition)

An abandoned church in a city named Sharon and the faith was Methodist – the church I was raised in! I examined the building and a cornerstone said, "Sharon." There were more than enough "signs" for me to know that the universe was providing and Julie and I just had to make something with this chance we were being given.

The man's wife came over to tell Julie and I that they had bought the old church, owned the property nearby and planned to tear it down since its abandoned state was attracting mayhem.

She also offered to let Julie and I tour the parson's house and the church. Dazed, we followed her into the adorable two-story home next door to the church. Inside, it was gutted out, a few piece of furniture or features left on the floor for someone to pick up and claim.

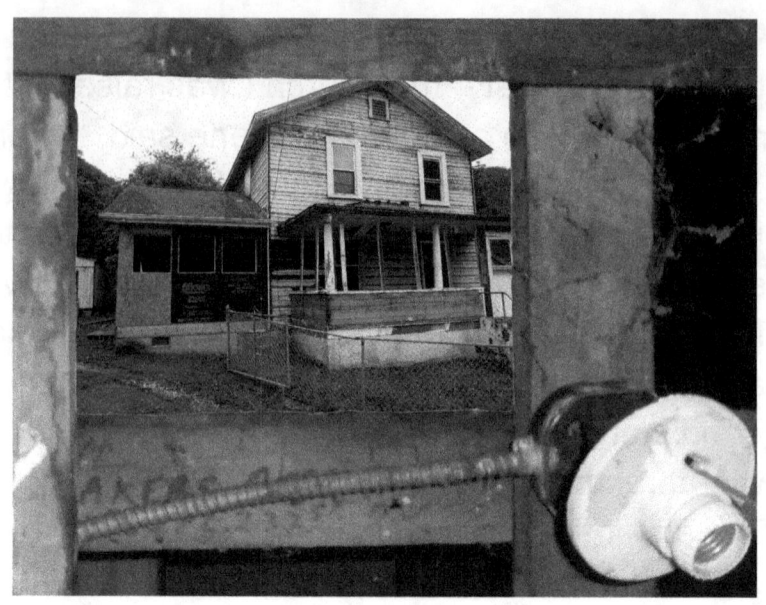

It had a classic layout with the stairway greeting one as they entered, a parlor to the side, an added on room. The landowner explained to us that the parson's widow had remained in the home in her ever-debilitating state. Relatives came and went, living with her, but she wanted to stay in the home she had known for so long. Reminders of her infirm condition were evident in an old hospital bed and appliances in a makeshift room on the bottom floor of the home. It reminded me of my mother who demanded she pass in her family home where her own mother had passed.

Julie elbowed me gently and nodded at the fireplace. I shook my head. The building was sagging, sad, peeling wallpaper, bugs settling in, and we were both

Abandoned Places: Abandoned Memories (Appalachian Edition)

in our heaven. The fireplace was charming and had been kept from view during many renovations.

Julie leaned into me and whispered, "Do you think she'll show us the church?"

I nodded hopefully.

Julie only half listened to the conversation, knowing that I would keep the woman engaged while she could focus on the photography. Getting the right angles, making use of the light through uncurtained windows was a challenge when presented with large expanses of empty rooms. She looked at the stairway and wondered if we would go upstairs. The building was so neglected that Julie wondered if the upstairs would support our weight.

As if our tour guide knew what we were hoping for, we ascended the stairwell. I eagerly awaited the tattered remaining rooms where sunlight would stream in uninterrupted by the church's imposing size next door. The building went from feeling riddled with pain and the debilitating state of the parson's wife, to feeling young and lived in. The woman explained some family had come and gone, staying there. I had a sense of little one toddling around in one of the bedrooms and the tone of this portion of the house felt more grounded in this world and less in the next world.

Julie clicked off pictures of the peeling wallpaper, the stripped fixtures, and the overall neglected surfaces.

And, then the woman offered to take us over to the church.

In my mind, I was thinking "Wow! Wow! Wow!" And, in Julie's mind, she was scrambling with her camera to get the best settings as the woman guided us first into the church's basement filled with covered boxes and furniture.

"One of the parson's family members left her things here. She has to get them out before we tear down." The woman explained. "We can't leave these buildings abandoned here. They just attract the wrong activities and elements."

We understood why they were compelled to remove the buildings for safety reasons, but part of me was thinking "can I have the cornerstone with my name on it and the bell and bell tower?" Of course, there was no way to move such things across country without enormous effort and expense, and the woman assured me that someone had offered on the bell. I was glad it was going to someone. If I had the building, I would have sawed off the bell tower with the bell and placed it in a garden, allowing ivy to take over. It would have been a gothic feature with a wonderful energy. It would have sat in the same spot as the church had for so long, left as a reminder of the sight of weddings and funerals, christenings and communions.

We took the creaking stairs up to the main floor where I was surprised to find many modern renovations that included a drop ceiling that was inappropriate for a classic clapboard church. The giant room didn't show any special ornamentation or even signs that it was a church.

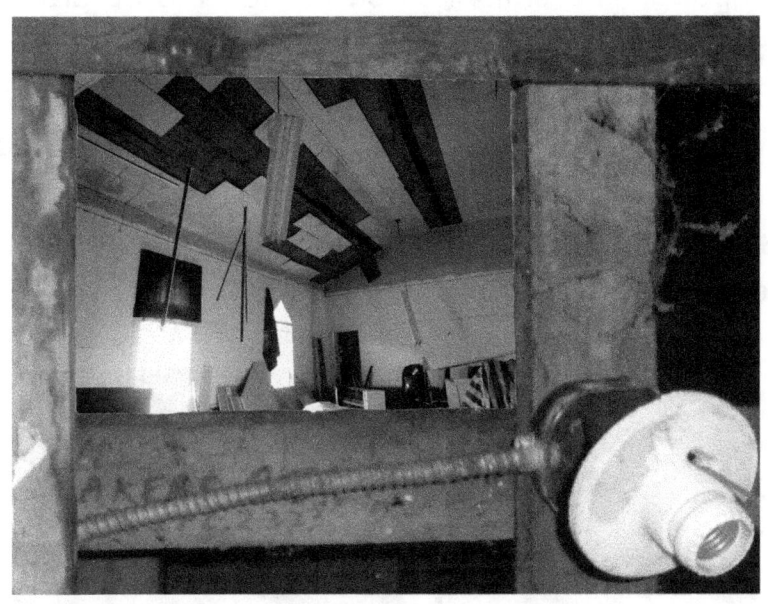

While Julie strived to take in the room, I noted the old church organ in the back corner, covered in a blanket. I pulled it back to take a peak and nodded to Julie. That was worth photographing!

The entryway had a sign that told of how many attended and how many collections were made. I thought to myself, "that would be so cool to have in my writer's

Abandoned Places: Abandoned Memories (Appalachian Edition)

office," but I have a tendency to collect too many things for an office that I have yet to construct.

I wedged myself into the narrow space where the bell pull and bell tower climb were located. Spider webs in the sunlight warned me not to go any further, but the sight was tempting. The child inside me that adored crawl spaces and hidden rooms was inspired.

In the main room of the church, I nodded to Julie that it was time for me to touch an object. When I did so and she took the photo, I locked onto a man that surprised and humbled me with his obstacles and his attitude....

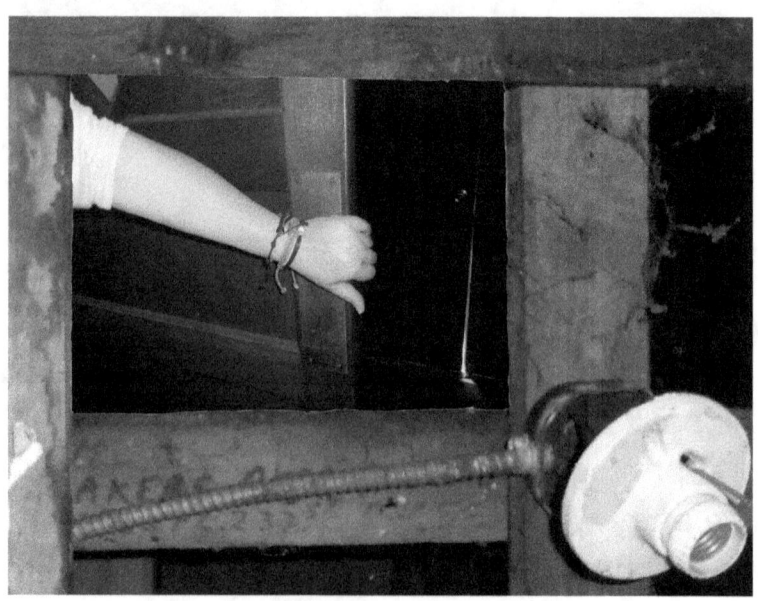

Abandoned Places: Abandoned Memories (Appalachian Edition)

A PURPOSEFUL LIFE

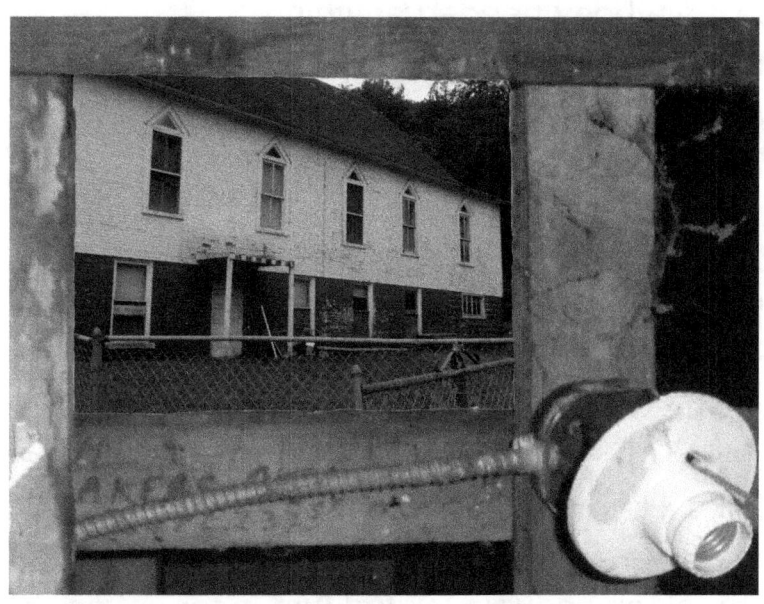

The world hadn't welcomed him like most. His parents were weak in the mind and he had come into the mix with his own mental and eventually emotional issues. Timid by nature and quiet, he was a respectful man. He didn't question dictates by his community, such as attending church or keeping the lawn mowed. He was the

Abandoned Places: Abandoned Memories (Appalachian Edition)

first to offer a strong hand when folks needed work done around their places. What he might have been deficient of in book learning, he more than made up for in strength and determination.

It had rained four days straight and the neighbors weren't coming out and that concerned him. Anything about the change in what was "normal" troubled him to the point that he needed to go out, cold and wet or not, and see if anybody needed anything.

The first door swung open and startled him. She must have been standing near the door.

"Y'all okay?"

"Hillside's slippin' again, but I think we have it handled. Got some sand bags up just in case. Reminds me of 97."

He nodded, not sure what 97 was. Then, it struck him that she was referring to the year. What happened in 97? He didn't have that kind of recall of storing years like some folks. He mumbled an agreement and moved on to the next house and the next.

The elderly couple invited him in for coffee, but he was dripping wet and didn't want to ruin their nice floor rug. He said he was busy and moved on back to his home, but not before having a look at the hillside. If he could, he'd hold it all back so it didn't threaten his neighbors, but he didn't have those kind of powers, as massive as his shoulders were.

Abandoned Places: Abandoned Memories (Appalachian Edition)

Back in his home, he dried off with a towel and threw some coal into the stove and watched out the windows for signs of people driving in and out. It felt like he was the last man on earth and that wasn't helping his nerves. He put on the radio and listened to the ever presence of some faithful hymns and rested back to drink some weak coffee while he watched the water streaking the windowpane and his breath and the hot coffee fogging it up.

He didn't hold a regular job. His parents had left him the house and their money, but his older sister helped to keep a watch on how he handled it. He never took money out at the bank and didn't really need anything other than some groceries. It ended up that more times than not his neighbors had him for supper or brought him things. He, in turn, split wood and fixed garden gates and the like. It worked well for him. His needs were few, except the need for companionship. That was always present.

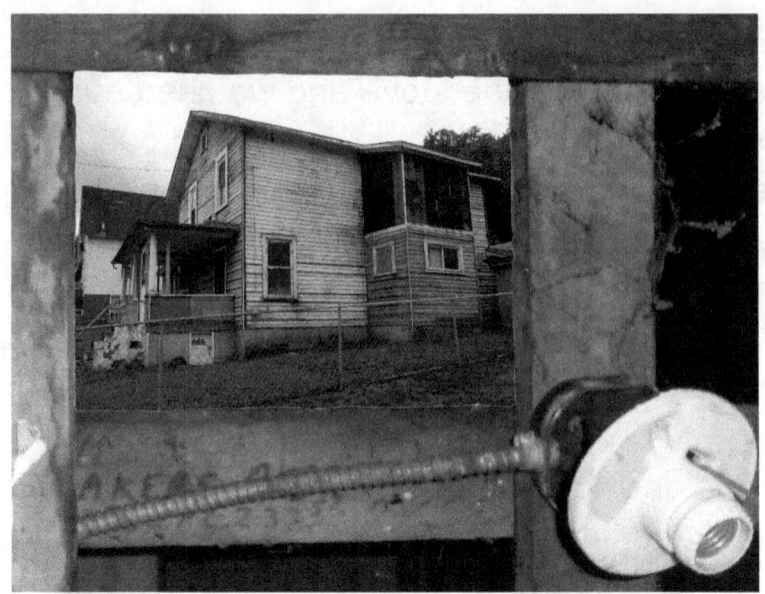

For a man who barely spoke, it was odd that he would hate being alone so much. He needed voices. He needed people around him, even if half the time he had to study what they said to understand some of the words and meanings. Like a visitor in a country where he barely spoke the language, he learned to just watch and listen and hope that he caught on. But, he never did quite catch on. His parents were bad examples of using their mental skills and even less so with the emotional. So, he safely kept himself neutral and was thankful that anyone wanted him around when he offered so little except his handy talents. Being needed was the purpose of his life.

Outside, a truck sloshed past down the narrow roadway towards the highway. He craned his neck to watch his neighbor leave. He wondered where he was

Abandoned Places: Abandoned Memories (Appalachian Edition)

going and who he was going with. Was he going off to hunt or fish? Probably not with all the rain. Maybe he was getting some supplies. It was about time to head into town and get groceries. He did that on Tuesdays with the elderly couple. They were kind enough to let him come along and he helped by unloading their groceries for them. It usually resulted in a supper there. For a man who was alone in the world, he had a fair deal of social life.

Sundays helped the most. The church needed him. He would do any task others were not rushing to volunteer. Other than being awful at cooking potluck meals, the upkeep of the building and the mowing of the grounds were simple enough ways to pay back his faith.

The Lord watched out for him and he appreciated the time to talk to Him in church. The Reverend did a fine job of leading them in prayers. And, he knew they were answered because he and his neighbors were happy, even when bad things happened, they circled around to help out and offer comfort. And Heaven allowed for all the good people to rejoin in a beautiful comforting place. He also knew some day he would join his parents and his uncles and aunts. His time on earth was one of service.

Abandoned Places: Abandoned Memories (Appalachian Edition)

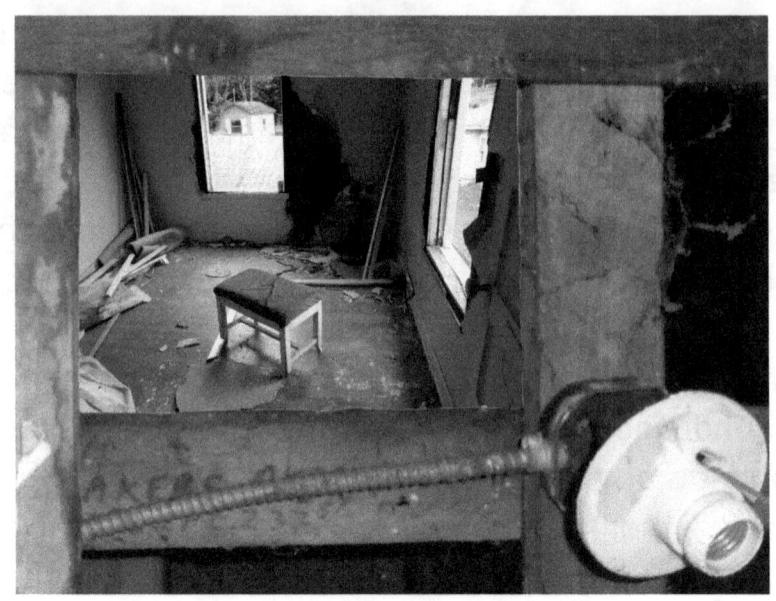

A knock on the door interrupted a sad song on the radio and he got up, straightening his shirt, smoothing the hairs on his head, hoping to not look too sloppy. One of the powerful brothers who lived up the hill stood there in the peeking sunshine, still wet from the drips coming off the roof line.

"We got our truck stuck in the mud on the hill. Wench isn't workin'. Wanna help?"

The brother, his name long forgotten, turned and walked away, knowing he'd follow. And he did. Silently he kept pace with the stocky man as he headed up the roadway.

The other brother sat at the driver's seat, radio blaring, and screamed over the loud noise.

Abandoned Places: Abandoned Memories (Appalachian Edition)

"Just see if you can lift that rear corner."

The walking brother came around and pointed to the rear corner of the truck and the man settled in beside him, helping to lift. His first grip wasn't working so he readjusted until it clicked and he felt the truck move a bit. While the driver started the truck forward, the man felt the tire try to get a hold. A rock underneath the mud caught hold of the tread and the truck started to lurch forward. He nearly fell face down in the muck when it took off.

The brother jumped into the cab and called out a thank you. He didn't offer to drive him back home as the clouds closed in again, blocking the sun, and bringing more rain. So, he hiked down the hill, mud up to his knees, and hid on the back porch where he sneaked out of the dirty trousers and pushed the door open, backing inside, making sure that there was no one on the edge of the property to see him. He rushed inside, dumped the pants in the sink and went back to the bathroom to run a hot shower.

Feeling secure in the neighborhood being quiet and no one needing him right now, he took pleasure in the simple act of standing under hot water and letting it hit his bad shoulder. He had burned out all his joints over the years by doing more than he was capable of physically, but his size made up for other shortcomings. The Lord gave him a strong back and ability to fix things. That was a calling. He couldn't put a price on a man's purpose.

Twilight was approaching and he flicked on the back porch light, looking out for his little furry friends. The plates were laid out with kitten kibble and a saucer of milk. The cats in the area ran wild, refused to be tamed, but there were no City services for strays, so he made sure they were taken care of for life. It was no less than his family had done for him.

Without opening the door, he could peer out at an angle and see two black tails. He knew which cats those were. The orange one wasn't there. That bothered him. Two days in a row "Orangie" hadn't come to the porch. "Blackie 1," "Blackie 2" and "Patches" never missed meal, but sometimes Orangie went days before he came back and if he opened the door, Orangie would run away quickly. He was quite a wild cat.

The lady across the way's granddaughter stood on their porch watching the cats being fed. He had tried to let her come over and pet them, but the woman seemed rather protective. It was a strange feeling he got from certain folks. They didn't want him near their children. Just because he didn't have any, didn't mean he didn't like them. They were little people, after all. And, he understood their curiosity and their feelings of not being allowed to do "important stuff."

Abandoned Places: Abandoned Memories (Appalachian Edition)

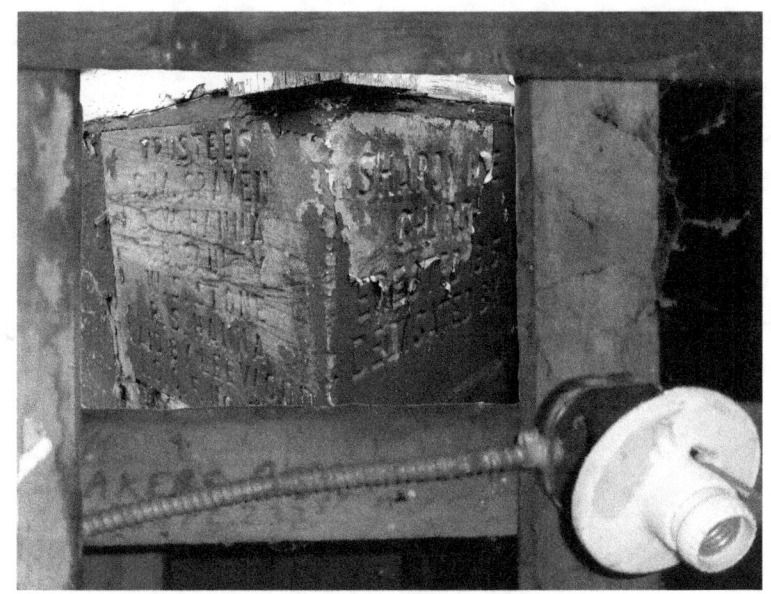

A car backfired and the cats darted off in terror for the woods again. The rain stopped. The darkness was closing in quickly. He went to the front window and looked out at the car across the street. Relatives were unloading for a Saturday supper. His belly grumbled and he thought about what there was to eat. It was going to be a soup and crackers night. It didn't seem anyone was coming to ask him over or bring him an extra casserole. He sighed and walked away, turning the radio off and turning on the TV instead. It was six o'clock. It was time for his Saturday night date and she never turned him down.

He flipped the channel until it settled on an attractive newswoman.

Abandoned Places: Abandoned Memories (Appalachian Edition)

"Hello Ms Marcus." He nodded his head at the screen.

She didn't respond, of course, but in his mind, he had his companionship over his bowl of soup. She didn't care if he wore his dress trousers or wiped his chin as he ate and she never ever called him names.

His dream date for six years, now, going on seven.

BONUS
ARE CEMETERIES HAUNTED?

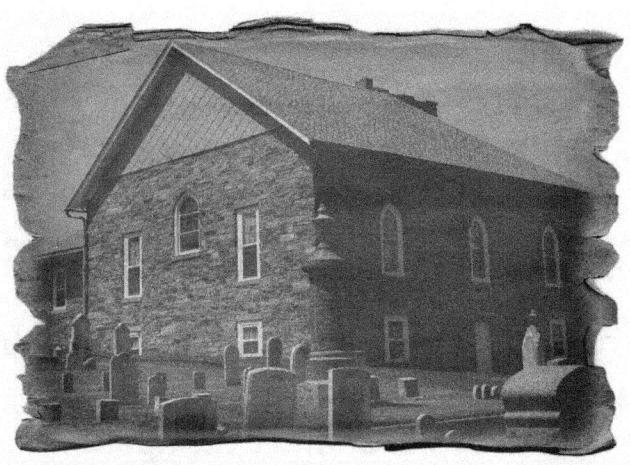

Why would ghosts hang around their dead bodies?

As a paranormal investigator, I'm asked this a lot and, in fact, when I first started investigating, I thought it was a ridiculous assumption. Cemeteries represent the dead, so we think that they must be creepy and haunted.

As I began to perform studies in cemeteries, though, I found something rather interesting; they do have activity. *Frequently*.

Why is this? I studied the cemeteries, noting that activity followed paths often used by people; roadways, walkways, straight lines. In the study of Feng Shui, a cemetery is considered to carry bad energy and energy

Abandoned Places: Abandoned Memories (Appalachian Edition)

likes to move in straight paths according to ancient Chinese studies. That might be a possible explanation for where you see activity, but the real question is, *why?*

It goes something like this. You spend the entire year surviving the loss of a loved one, yet again. Anniversary comes around and you go to their grave. You sit down, have a little talk with the deceased cherished person, cry, remember, wish, hope they hear you. Then, you leave. The spirit comes to those who call on it. In your own grief and mini-séance, you called up on the dead to visit. They might have been over your right shoulder, pressing a hand to offer comfort. And, when you leave, activity shows up around that spot for some time.

I have found this over and over again when visiting a graveyard, the newly visited graves have activity, whether it's voices, shadows, or full apparitions. I believe the only way you can incite a spirit to make a connective form is through a living human. We are conduits of a sort which might also explain our propensity for psychokinesis (moving objects by thought) and poltergeist activity.

As well, cemeteries are often times visited by shadow people. These 3-4 foot tall, human shaped, completely dense and black figures dart around headstones and pathways and if a person looks them straight on, they disappear as if they are alarmed they were caught. Why would a cemetery be a spot for such entities?

Abandoned Places: Abandoned Memories (Appalachian Edition)

There are a lot of theories including they are guardians of the dead, spirit forms of the dead trying to materialize, other dimensional beings interested in visiting, but choosing less traveled places to observe, and projections of our own minds. Whatever these figures are, they are extremely unsettling for those who witness them and leave a lifetime of questions about the paranormal. It can often be the catalyst for a person becoming what Julie and I referred to in our book, "Paranormal Geeks."

I often tell people that if they have some moments utterly alone, to call on a deceased loved one and talk to them, ask for advice, ask for comfort. Pay special attention to how you feel in your body – where in your body? How? In your mind/heart - how do they manifest? A scent? A pat? A feeling of presence? Start to learn the way you feel that loved one. Then, you will always have an insight into when they are with you and who is with you.

Every time I'm at a cemetery, I find the very old unattended graves, ones who passed so long ago that anyone that knew them is also gone. I read their name out loud. I read their headstone. I say hello. And, I leave a flower. I also bring trash bags in the trunk of my car in case I happen upon a cemetery, I bring one with me and pick up anything left behind to keep it beautiful. They are very much like quiet parks, but parks for the soul.

It is impossible to leave a cemetery and not walk away thinking about your own mortality and the time left on the clock. What do you want on your headstone? What would you regret doing? Or, more importantly, what would you regret *not* doing?

CHAPTER FIVE
ABANDONED TOWNHOUSES

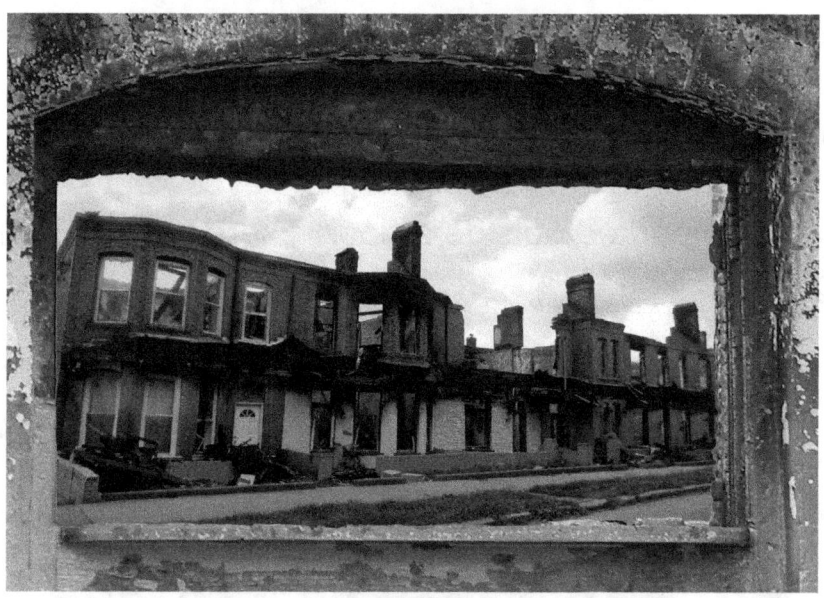

Julie and I did not expect to find this place. We were rolling along the side streets of a small railroad town along a riverfront and checking out the charming cottage houses nestled on the hillside when our eyes caught sight of a massive burned out beast, taking up an entire block. The burned out townhouses still smelled heavily of charcoal.

Curious about this tragically beautiful edifice, we stopped the car, climbed out and took a stroll. The back side of the building had burned out and dropped away and you could see the beautiful mountain in the distance through the windows.

Julie rushed up and down the sidewalk, getting as many angles as possible, but both of us remained silent. It was on both our minds. Had anyone been hurt? Why hadn't they secured it from children wandering in and getting hurt? How did it get started?

She tried to ignore it, but Julie's eyes kept settling on a stroller parked outside a door. There were children living here. Did they all get out?

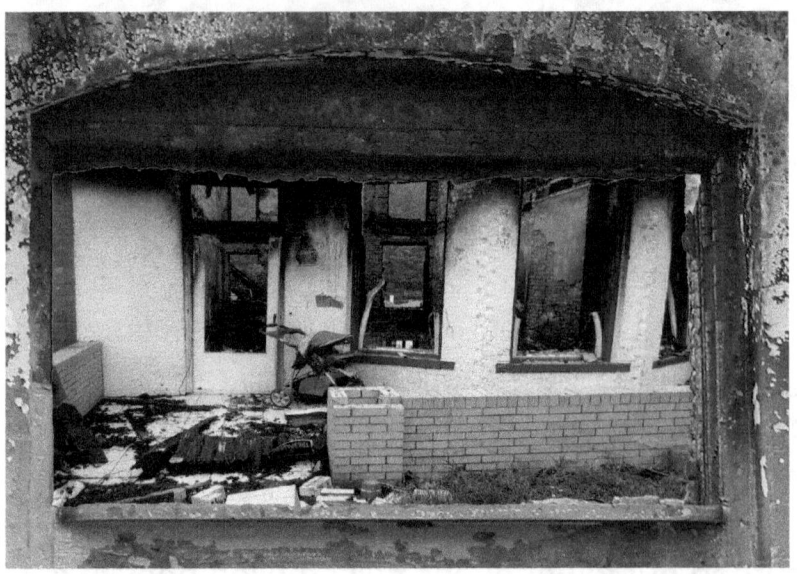

Framing the pictures was easy with all the architecture, windows and doors laid bare. Julie squinted up at the angled sun upon the row houses and tried to guess where the fire started. It seemed like the middle unit, since it was most damaged.

Julie remarked, "Look at that shelf in the corner – still has its dishes on it and nothing left around it."

It was chilling.

There was something morbid about hovering around the remains of people's homes where they brought home babies and brides, had fights and make-ups, grieved loses, celebrated anniversaries, and children laid down their childhood memories. What memories would they have now?

Julie shook her head. "I just hope everyone made it out."

"Me too." I agreed.

I lifted my camera and took photos too, hoping to capture something that hovered around in the back of my mind, the beauty of the greenery on the mountain as seen through the charred barren windows. It was breathtaking the colorless charcoal sill and the vibrant neon greens of the early summer growth. In a strange poignant way, it reminded me of the untouched life all around the building that once held so much life, as well. Within seconds, any of it could go under the danger of a flame and lose all its vitality and industry, both the building and the forest.

We were reminded instantly of the fragility of our own lives, possessions, and homes.

Abandoned Places: Abandoned Memories (Appalachian Edition)

I nodded to Julie, letting her know I was ready to do a reading and stepped forward to grab a doorknob. As always, I had no idea if I would get the last person who touched it, the person who touched it the most, or someone who had simply touched it at one point or another and left an impression that I caught in my mind's eyes. It was always a crap shoot as to whose content on the item I interpreted.

I gathered both male and female energy, but even though the male's was easier to read, the female's energy intrigued me much more because she was the one affected by his charismatic energy. I then focused myself on her and she unfolded like a Phoenix rising from the ashes of the townhome.

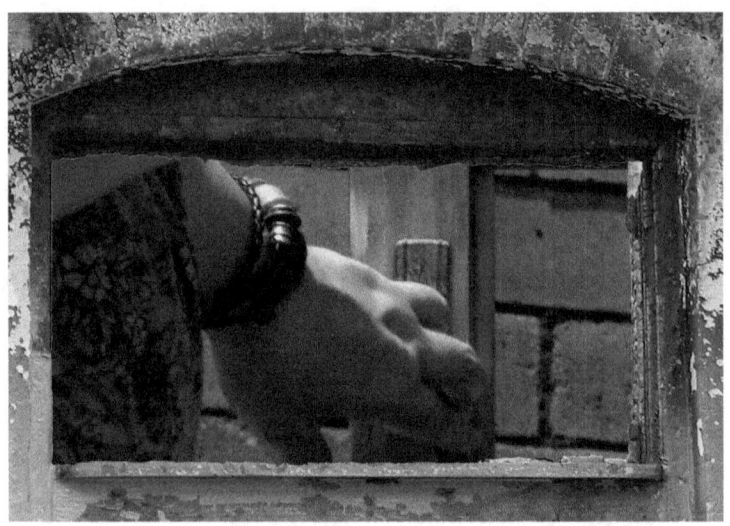

Abandoned Places: Abandoned Memories (Appalachian Edition)

RUNNING FROM THE PAST

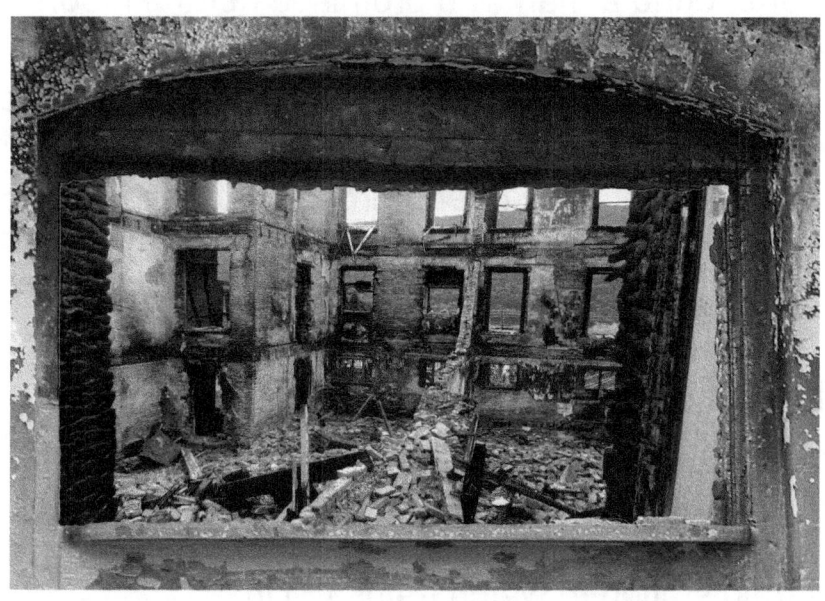

She had three long-term relationships by the age of 31; each one producing a son. Her first impulsive decision was to leave home at 17, but that was because she had enough of arguing with her mom and her mom's new husband patting her butt.

She moved in with her first real boyfriend, Randy, when he graduated high school. They lived in his parents' house and had their baby when she was just 18. That lasted until their boy was 2 and then Randy decided he wanted another girl. As awkward as that was, she stayed in the home while she dated another man and he dated another woman. The grandparents spoiled their boy rotten just like they had their own son, causing him to be a bit of a tyrant.

She found a man who promised her the moon, talked big about making it in the world and getting out of their town. They met at her sister's barbecue. He was 10 years older than her at all of 31 years and she moved in with him fast. He didn't offer marriage after six years and one baby boy. But, he did at least hold a job and make it possible to rent a little house near the river.

His dreams were shelved for the reality of work and he often took two or three jobs at a time. It wasn't easy watching him come and go and leave her alone with the boys, but she did enjoy chasing butterflies with them, walking around the river looking for pretty rocks and going to the train station to watch trains roll in.

And, he brought home money and fixed things around the house, but he never really enjoyed talking. He excessively enjoyed making love, though. He nearly wore her out with his moods. Sometimes, it would take him over and she could barely walk for a week. It was the only time he showed affection, so she would take it when she could. Otherwise, he was busy on the phone, reading the paper, or coming and going.

Abandoned Places: Abandoned Memories (Appalachian Edition)

A few times, she suspected he wasn't where he said he was and she'd call his night job to find he wasn't on that night. So where was he all those hours?

It ate at her like cancer until from the moment she woke up alone until she went to bed alone, she had images of him laughing about his woman and kids at home and rolling around in bed with someone she likely knew; someone in their small town. She wanted to follow him, but she had no car. Stranded in the house by the river with the young ones, she was just lucky that someone was taking care of her. After all, she barely finished high school on average grades and never held a job.

Insecurity ate at her until one night when he came home, obviously drunk. She'd never seen him drunk before. Like a different man, his face twisted, and he spat when he spoke, leaning into her face, stabbing a finger at her, telling her why his life sucked and he hated it. And, she and their son and his stepson were all part of those things.

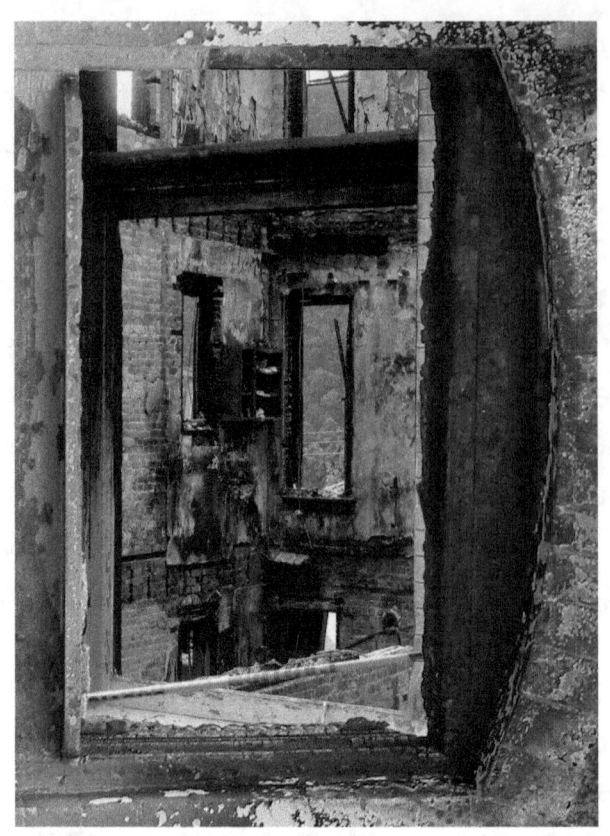

He didn't remember it the next day, or maybe he didn't want to acknowledge it. She couldn't go back home. Her mother wanted her nowhere near her husband. So, she continued on there, the empty shell of a partner going through the motions. And, he avoided her like a punished child or perhaps a sulking one.

Then, one day, she ran into Brian, from high school, in the local drug store. She had walked with the boys into downtown and wanted to get some candy when he came up the aisle and smiled at the boys first and then her.

Abandoned Places: Abandoned Memories (Appalachian Edition)

"They're cute." Brian patted the baby's head.

And she smiled dumbly at him.

They started talking about what happened since school and he was being groomed for a position in his father's business in town to take over when his father retired. She was impressed. And, he was smiling as much as she was. It was a goofy feeling. Not at all like the lust of her first love or the way she had been impressed with the older man in her second relationship. This man made her feel something all together different, almost untouched by all her experiences.

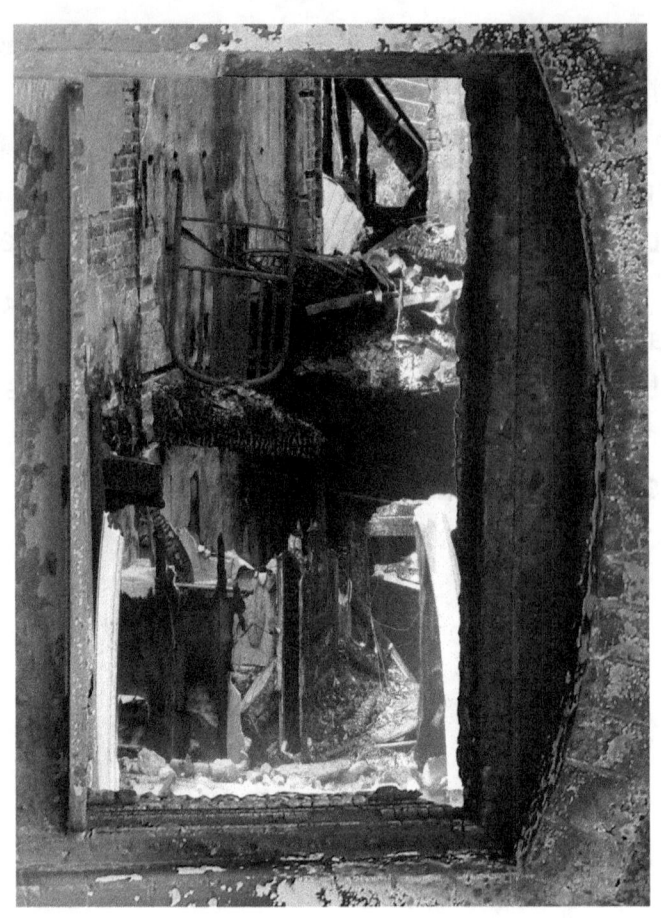

Knowing her situation was uncomfortable and wishing her out of the home with Man #2, Brian set her up with a place of her own and within weeks she was moved into her own place with her babies and Brian was madly in love with her. He paid her bills, brought her gifts, and spent most of his nights there. Months went by and she felt like they were family, except the nights he went to his own place to sleep. It seemed silly for him to have two homes, but she assumed he was preparing his family for the news that he had found someone and didn't want to be living together when they should be married.

Eagerly, she awaited his visits.

His handsome face lit up, his eyes sparkled and he always took the time to greet the boys and sometimes get on the floor and roll around, letting them climb all over him. When the boys were all ready for bath and bed, then it was their time. He always knew exactly when to arrive for them to have time as a family and time alone. On nights he left early, he slipped out of bed by 11 and kissed her goodbye.

He hadn't said he loved her yet, but that was quite obvious. She hadn't said it either. Perhaps there was some residual fear that every time she had said that word, relationships changed. It was endearing to her that they were both afraid. They could be afraid together and find a safe place in each other's arms.

In the back of her mind, she recalled that he didn't take her out to supper. He brought supper sometimes or she cooked it, but they never went out in public. He supposed it was his worry about how everyone talks so readily. Soon, others would bother them about when they were setting a wedding date and she certainly didn't want him to feel forced.

She tried not to look at the fact they spent almost all their time together in bed or that he paid her bills but did not live there. Months kept ticking by without any signs from him that he was ready to ask the question.

And then, one day, she knew without a doubt she was pregnant. The set of signs were impossible to ignore. He had used a condom for some time and got tired of using them and she tried to evaluate her periods to know the safest times to make love, but the inevitable had happened. He loved her boys so she anticipated telling him the news and perhaps seeing him speed up the relationship a bit.

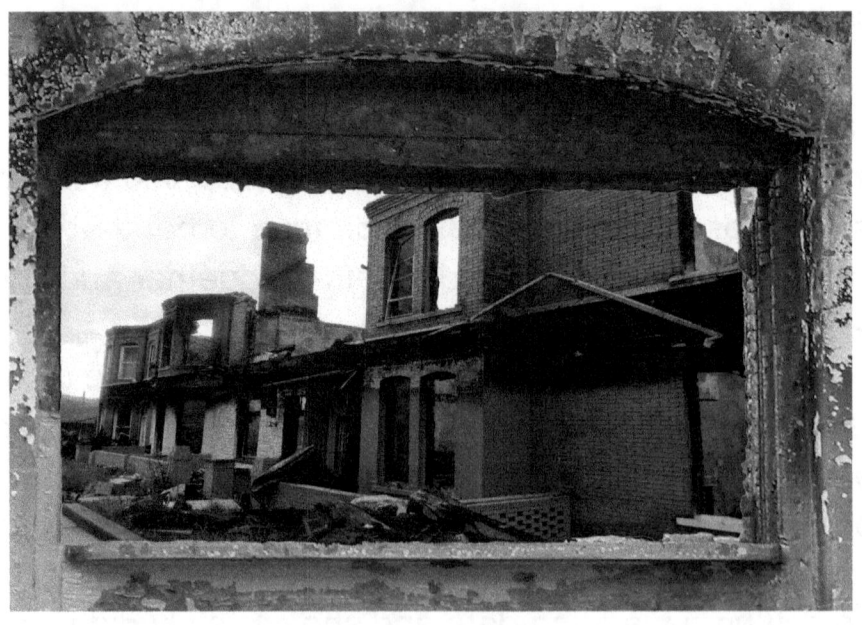

She told Brian she had something important to tell him and suddenly he was busy every day for eight days in a row. Then, when he did show up, he brought

Abandoned Places: Abandoned Memories (Appalachian Edition)

champagne and candy and apologized profusely and she forgot about all insecurities.

They were sprawled out in bed in the glorious aftermath of missing each other and she leaned her head against his shoulder and told him. In his usual considerate manner he asked.

"Did I hurt you? Both of you?" He put his hand on her shoulder and pulled her in and she laughed. Why had she worried at his reaction?

"We're fine." She giggled.

He kissed her forehead, got up to go to the bathroom and took a long time.

"Feeling kind of exhausted, baby." He told her. "I should get moving. I need to be to work early, so I'm going to sleep at home."

She pulled the sheet up around her, suddenly cold. He referred to his place as home.

"Okay." She agreed.

He kissed her lips warmly and then dressed and let himself out.

The pregnancy moved along just fine and he visited as he usually had. He came after dark now and his car was parked down the street. She did notice that and wondered. She was showing so perhaps he was afraid people would realize he got her pregnant. It was too late to try to hide it at the altar and he wasn't getting close to asking for marriage or telling her he loved her or anything about the future.

He had no intentions of marrying her. She knew that after the delivery of their son. Three boys. Three different men. All of them with issues committing. She went through the motions when he visited, which he did less often. Inside she was numb. The depression following their son's birth was immense. He loved the baby quite obviously. But, he still parked his car down the street and went home to sleep each time he visited.

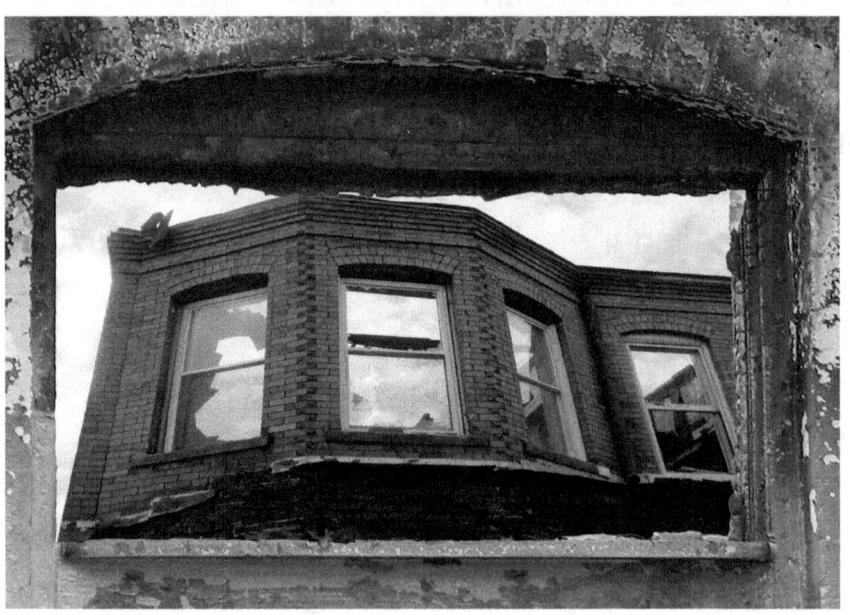

She might have been at her breaking point if her first love hadn't come back into her life, showing up to visit his son and seeming more confident in his mature self. He had a series of bad relationships and told her that he realized he threw away the best thing he ever had. He also figured out who her boyfriend was and became enraged that he would take advantage of her.

"He has no plans to marry you, ever. You know that? His parents would never allow it."

She nodded, tears filling her eyes.

Randy paced the floor and then dropped to his knee, taking her hand in his.

"I have no reason to think you'd ever say yes, but please at least consider marrying me."

"I-I can't possibly. I mean…"

He smiled and touched her cheek. "You think on it, baby doll. I am asking to make you legitimate and all our beautiful sons."

"All?" She blinked. He wanted to claim all her children?

He nodded.

She would have shown him out, but her knees weren't working. And she had another issue to finally face after almost two years. Even if Brian did offer to marry her, she couldn't stop thinking about her first.

And that, perhaps, he should be her last.

Abandoned Places: Abandoned Memories (Appalachian Edition)

BONUS

ABANDONED OBJECT
STUFFED ANIMAL
LOCATION CEMETERY

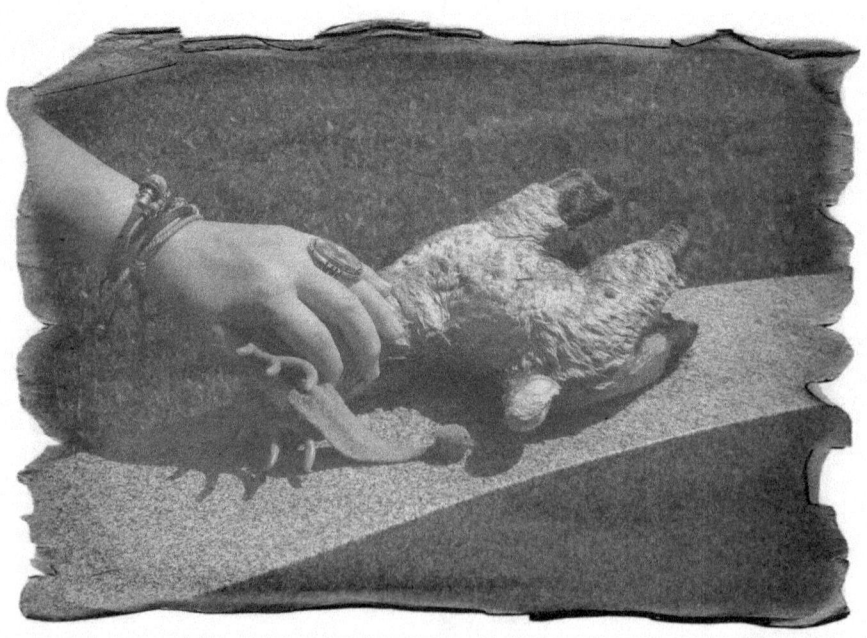

Abandoned Places: Abandoned Memories (Appalachian Edition)

As I touched the stuffed animal left on a grave in one of the most lovely cemeteries I have ever seen, I couldn't help feeling a blast of emotion and images in my mind. Rather than sort these into some interpretation, I will leave you with the images, words, feelings, and more that I saw flashing through my head. This is what a read is like and it takes deep interpretative skills to be able to form a coherent story when this is all out of context.

In other words, this list below represents how I made all these readings above into story form of a scene from the past, knowing all the things I did about the people and glimpses of their lives.

Woman.
Late 40s.
Mousy brown hair
"Let herself go,"
Husband not attracted to her
No communication
Blue eyes
Same day over and over again
Only half hears what people say
Mark and John
Belly clenched, never takes a deep breath
Escapes in playing piano
Isolation
Dark room

Abandoned Places: Abandoned Memories (Appalachian Edition)

Naps
Pacing
Aching bones
Deep gut-wrenching sobs
Watches the same 5 movies over and over
Education gone to waste

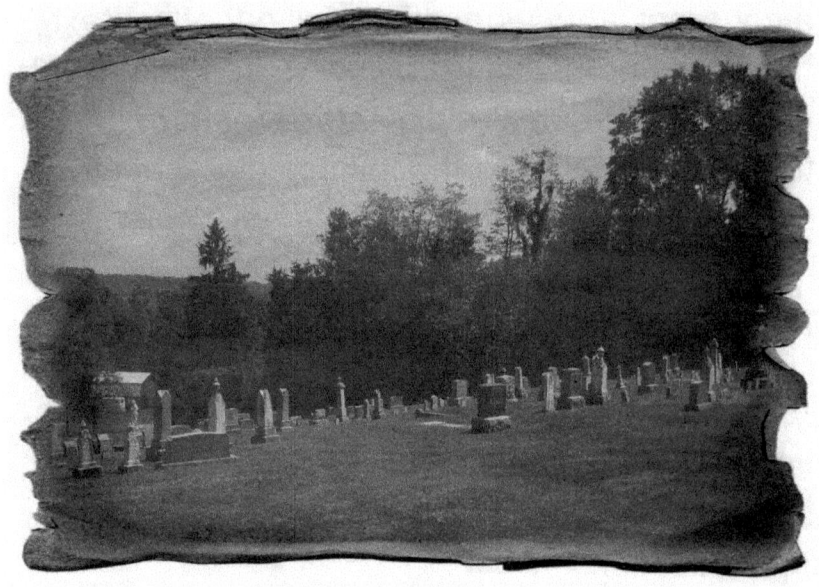

Abandoned Places: Abandoned Memories (Appalachian Edition)

CHAPTER SIX
ABANDONED FARMHOUSE

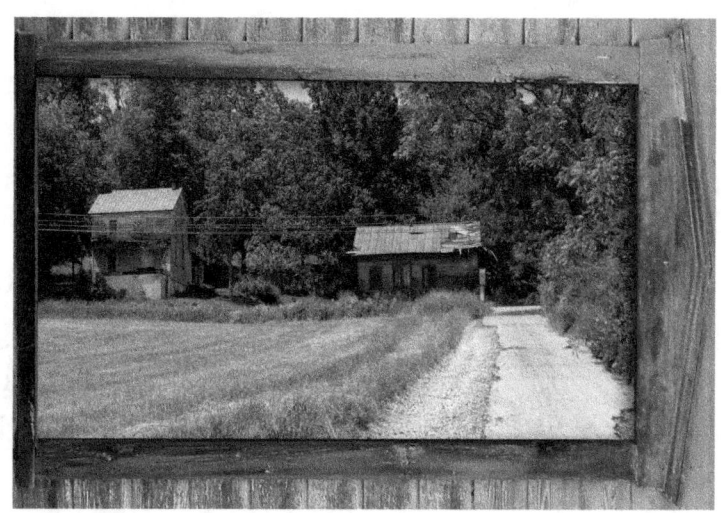

Julie and I meant to continue out trek into Pennsylvania but in extreme western Maryland, a sight in the distance had us pulling over to check it out. We parked the car in front of an overgrown long driveway and proceeded to walk up to the two abandoned buildings side by side. One was an impressive two-story clapboard and the other a little building that appeared to once be a cottage turned storage shed or some such use.

"Oh what I would give to go inside there!" I exclaimed as I studied the clapboard house. It was still a lovely farmhouse sight and had an upstairs veranda that was an interesting architectural feature. Someone had bothered to come in and mow the area around the buildings even though they remained unattended which confirmed that perhaps the neighbors were not happy to have abandoned sites nearby. In fact, the darling house I desperately wanted to go inside of had a "No Trespassing" sign that Julie and I always obeyed when we came across.

Julie wasn't sure what to photograph first. She went back and forth between the two buildings. The day was gorgeous and clear, the foliage bright green, wildflowers waving in the soft warm breeze, and not a car in sight. We both circled around looking at the drab little building and the romantic looking old clapboard house from all the angles, discovering something new with each glance.

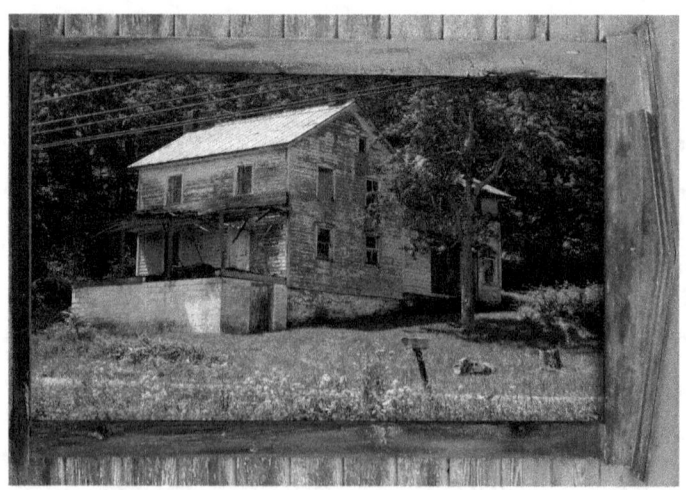

Abandoned Places: Abandoned Memories (Appalachian Edition)

I hadn't considered doing a read on these places at the time because I was hoping to find an abandoned building with a really unusual purpose and we had already done the bridge house reading, but something about the older building on the property kept drawing me back.

Maybe it was the utilitarian look of it or the fact that it had some lingering essence of one individual in particular whereas the house seemed to exude a calliope of characters in its history.

Out of curiosity, I reached out and touched the building, caressing anything metal that had a better chance of retaining information. I stepped back, took some photos, stepped forward, touched again. I tapped into someone who had touched the building and his mind haunted me. I felt like I knew him. He sort of reminded me of my Uncle Arlie. I stepped up, touched again and Julie clicked off a picture.

"Is this going to be a read?" She asked.

I nodded dumbly. It had chosen me this time.

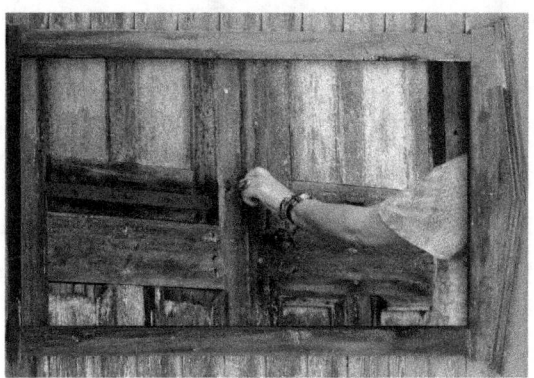

Abandoned Places: Abandoned Memories (Appalachian Edition)

TOO MANY DAUGHTERS

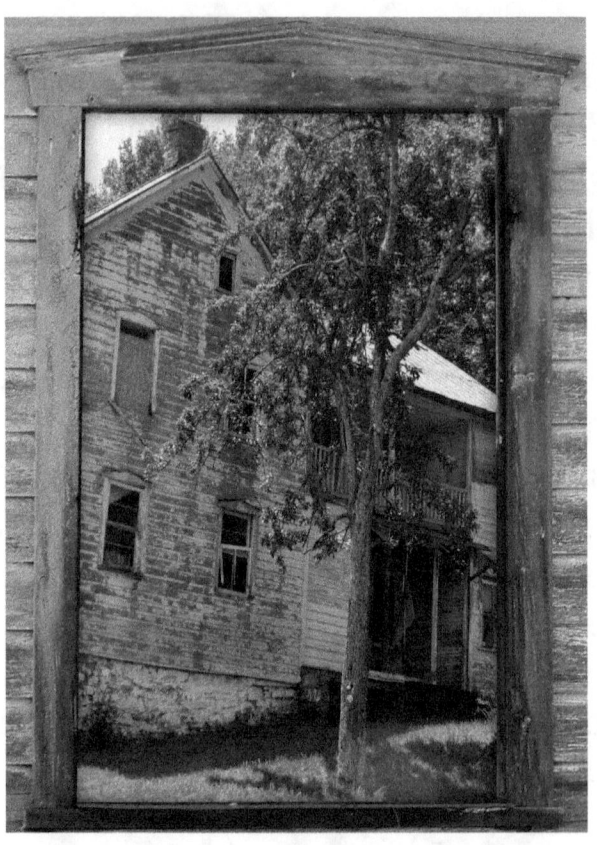

The land was good. The neighbors were fine. The wood was sturdy. The construction was tight. And the man took pride in the fact he had made this all come together in a fine piece of property. In fact, the Good Lord

Abandoned Places: Abandoned Memories (Appalachian Edition)

had given him nearly everything he could need, except for the one thing he had wanted his whole life.

Sons.

He sighed and stepped back to study the alignment of the door on the threshold. His wife had complained about the drafts, but it was part of the life on a hill with a pasture that didn't stop the steady stream of chill autumn air.

The smell of wood smoke combined with the earthy mushrooms and molding leaves. He had just raked up yet another pile of leaves to burn, but it would keep. Tonight, he had to move the potatoes into the root cellar and get the horses in the barn for the first frost.

He bent over to pick up his tools when he heard his oldest daughter screaming from an upstairs window for her twin sister to stay out of her things. He shook his head and walked away, hoping no one saw him out the window. He was often asked to calm down the hysterics between his five daughters and it was more than any man should have to endure when his wife chimed in, her voice a bit deeper and louder. He could never focus on who to calm down first, so he opted to tiptoe away as they screamed.

He made it into the workshop, his getaway from all the females. This was his place. The wood still smelled like wood, not wallpaper and tea. It was a man's place. It suited protection from the elements and offered few places for cold to seep in through the thick walls.

Once the door closed, few came to try and find him. It was a great retreat. He could neither hear the fighting next door or the icy turn of the wet air outside. He laid his tools down on the sturdy work table and lit the lantern, going back to arrange the tools in their proper places so he could find them by memory, even without lighting the light.

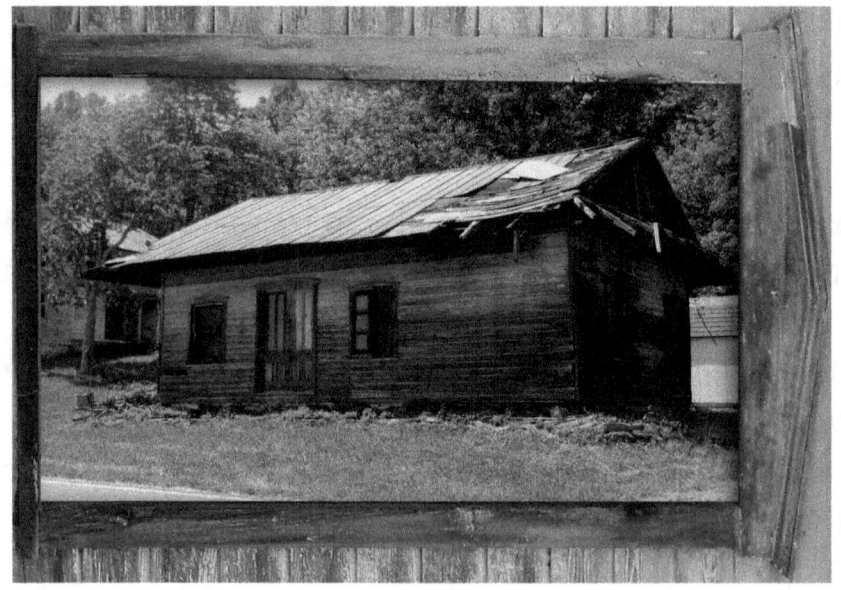

He picked up a bushel of potatoes freshly picked, the earthy dirt scent of them reaching his nose and then he recalled his childhood in a rush of memories. His Irish parents, new to the country, had insisted on growing potatoes and marveled every time the crops came in. They truly believe America was the land of magic and they would never face hardship again. It was too bad they had both passed before their 42nd birthdays.

The man shoved the door aside with his elbow and stepped back into the cold air, closed his eyes, took a breath of the wet smoky air and proceeded to head to the house. He set the basket down as he reached for the door, but one of his daughters swung it open in, hand on her hip, looking as if he were late to her communion.

It was the second to the youngest. She was just like her mama.

"Mom said supper is ready in 20 minutes. You better not be late again, daddy. She's gonna pop a button."

Admittedly, that sass made him snort with humor. His wife used to be like that. Last several years she was just more and more quiet and when she did speak, she meant it, in utterly humorless form.

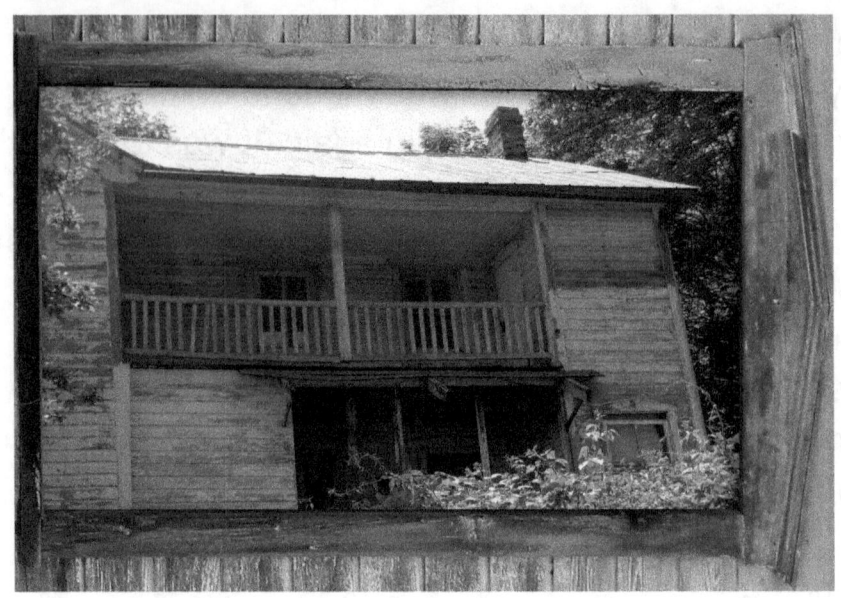

Not surprising him, his daughter took the bushel from him. "I'll take it down, daddy. You get the other one."

He nodded and without a word thankfully stepped back outside again. She was a special one. He hoped to God that she didn't let life wear her down into a tightly wound, resentful, shell of a woman like his wife. He meant to keep her spunk ever present and her resilience and kindness fresh as always. The other daughters were foreign to him, but this one was his hope.

The lantern still glowed inside his workshop. The man went over and hoisted the last bushel of potatoes up and set it on the table, went to the far side of the room and looked at the rocking chair his grandmother once rocked his father in when he was a baby in Ireland. His wife said it didn't fit near their hearth. She wouldn't use it to rock their babies. Sometimes, when she held one of the girls and rocked them as she stood near the fire, he saw a strange expression on her face, a kind of smirk, as if she were so happy to present him with yet another girl.

It wasn't a reasonable assumption, but he couldn't shake the sense that his wife didn't like getting pregnant every couple years and was pleased he retreated away from the chaos. In her own way, she was in her element cooking and teaching the girls to sew and fussing over their hair styling, but the relationship with them grew and with him, faded.

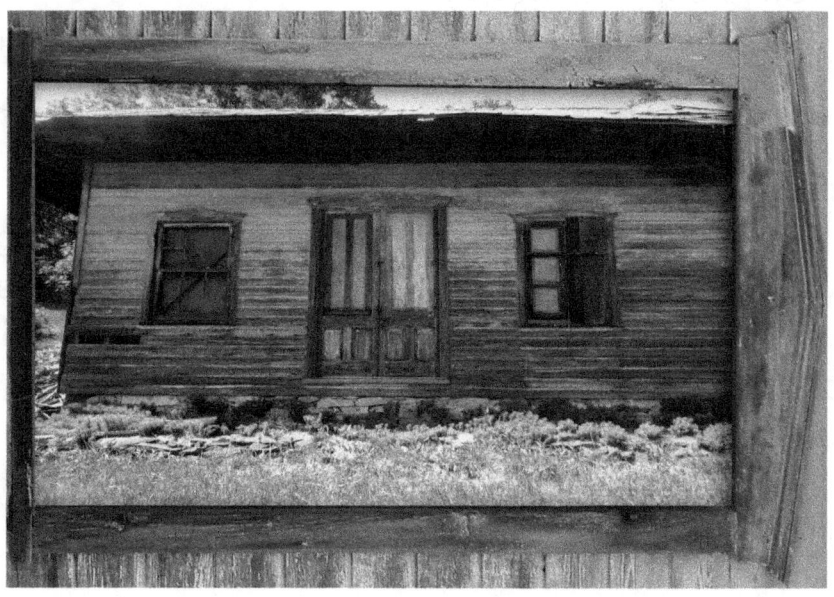

Abandoned Places: Abandoned Memories (Appalachian Edition)

He dilly dallied as long as he could before he went back into the house with the last of the potatoes and a full night of women folk. When he elbowed the front door open and closed it against the chill wet air, he found a clear path to the basement with no women in the way.

Emily still lingered down in the chilly dry recesses of the root cellar area, pushing aside baskets and making room for the rest of the potatoes.

"Tomorrow, will you show me how to use the tiller?"

He chuckled.

She remained silent.

"You mean that?" He asked her.

She nodded earnestly.

He patted her fair head. "I'll make a farmer of you yet."

"I certainly hope so, daddy." She grinned and marched upstairs proudly.

The future showed some promise. If one of the girls didn't marry a handy man who wanted to take over the property, at least this little one would be sure and take pride in it as he had done. She showed interest in lots of boyish deeds.

If one wasn't going to have a son, at least he could produce a daughter-farmer.

Abandoned Places: Abandoned Memories (Appalachian Edition)

CLOSING

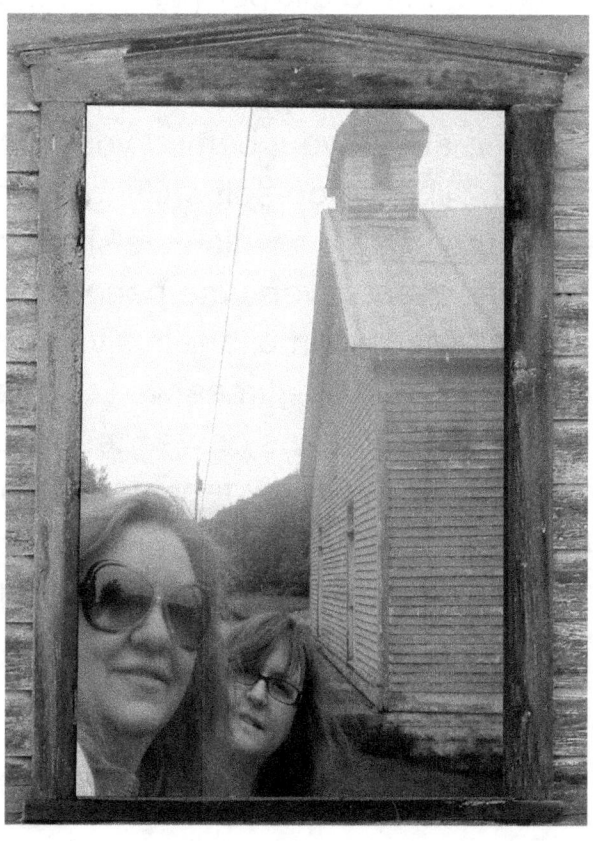

Julie and I spend a good deal of our free time exploring places that have been forgotten, historic landmarks, haunted locations, and more. But, one thing that we find most gratifying about this book series is being able to document places that may no longer exist and are fast being plowed under or destroyed by time and decay. We also find it rewarding to reveal that, no matter how dead a building may appear, how far from its original glory, it still contains the souls of those who entered there. It is on the surfaces, in the air, permeating the very space in which you stand.

If you close your eyes and feel the place, becoming aware of the space above you, behind you, to the right, left and front, you will find yourself shifting ever so slightly into that space – the space in which we share every moment with every event, even time period, every person who inhabited that space. Simultaneously, we are all together and that is how sometimes we tap this information by "psychic" means or we feel goosebumps and don't know why or suddenly feel melancholy but can't explain what changed.

We encourage others to explore safely and to especially explore *the sharing of the space*.

Abandoned Places: Abandoned Memories (Appalachian Edition)

www.ingramcontent.com/pod-product-compliance
Lightning Source LLC
Chambersburg PA
CBHW051323170526

45166CB00002B/665